MAYER SMITH

The Runaway Bride

Copyright © 2025 by Mayer Smith

All rights reserved. No part of this publication may be reproduced, stored or transmitted in any form or by any means, electronic, mechanical, photocopying, recording, scanning, or otherwise without written permission from the publisher. It is illegal to copy this book, post it to a website, or distribute it by any other means without permission.

This novel is entirely a work of fiction. The names, characters and incidents portrayed in it are the work of the author's imagination. Any resemblance to actual persons, living or dead, events or localities is entirely coincidental.

Mayer Smith asserts the moral right to be identified as the author of this work.

Mayer Smith has no responsibility for the persistence or accuracy of URLs for external or third-party Internet Websites referred to in this publication and does not guarantee that any content on such Websites is, or will remain, accurate or appropriate.

Designations used by companies to distinguish their products are often claimed as trademarks. All brand names and product names used in this book and on its cover are trade names, service marks, trademarks and registered trademarks of their respective owners. The publishers and the book are not associated with any product or vendor mentioned in this book. None of the companies referenced within the book have endorsed the book.

First edition

This book was professionally typeset on Reedsy. Find out more at reedsy.com

Contents

1	The Perfect Wedding	1
2	Great Disappearance	7
3	New Identity	15
4	Meeting the Writer	24
5	Normal Life	32
6	First Spark	40
7	Secrets and Stories	49
8	Hidden Truth	56
9	Investigator's Shadow	63
10	A Game of Shadows	71
11	The Confrontation	78
12	The Escape	85
13	The Truth	91
14	The Betrayal	98
15	Into the Abyss	105
16	Escape Plan	112
17	The Brink of Darkness	119
18	Final Stand	126
19	Brink of Betrayal	133
20	Breaking Point	141

One

The Perfect Wedding

Vivienne Sinclair stared at her reflection in the ornate, gilded mirror, her face an unblemished portrait of perfection. Her dark brown hair cascaded in soft waves over her shoulders, styled meticulously by the best hands money could buy. Her makeup was impeccable, her lips a delicate shade of rose, her eyes lined just enough to accentuate their striking green color. The wedding dress—hand-stitched with pearls and embroidered with the finest lace from Paris—hugged her slender frame as if it had been sculpted onto her. It was breathtaking.

And she hated every inch of it.

A sickly tightness gripped her chest, making it difficult to breathe. The lace choked her, the fabric suffocated her, and the massive diamond ring on her finger felt like a shackle, weighing her hand down.

The clock on the antique wooden mantelpiece struck ten. Two hours until she walked down the aisle, two hours until she became Mrs. Ethan Harrington.

A soft knock on the door made her flinch.

"Vivienne, darling?" Her mother's voice, smooth and polished, seeped through the heavy oak door. "The guests are starting to arrive. Are you ready?"

Vivienne swallowed, trying to steady her voice. "Almost, Mother."

The handle turned, but Vivienne was already at the door, keeping it shut with her palm. "I just need a moment."

There was a pause before her mother sighed. "You've had years to prepare for this, dear. It's a bit late for hesitation."

Yes. Years. Years of being molded into the perfect Sinclair daughter, the flawless heiress, the woman fit for a billionaire's wife.

She closed her eyes, leaning against the door, listening as her mother's heels clicked away down the hall. The sound felt like the ticking of a clock, marking the countdown to her inevitable fate.

Two hours.

The Perfect Wedding

She had to act now.

Vivienne moved quickly, stepping over the sea of white fabric as she lifted the hem of her dress and made her way toward the vanity. She yanked open a drawer and retrieved a pair of scissors. With a sharp inhale, she raised them to her hair.

One precise snip, then another.

Dark strands tumbled onto the gleaming marble floor, scattering around her feet. Each cut felt like a tiny rebellion, a piece of herself breaking free. When she finished, her long, elegant locks were no more—her hair now framed her face in a messy, shoulder-length bob.

Her heart pounded. No going back now.

She rushed to the closet and grabbed the duffel bag she had hidden days ago, filled with simple clothes, cash, and a burner phone she had secretly purchased online. She tore off the suffocating wedding gown and slipped into a pair of jeans and a black hoodie. The transformation was drastic, but it wasn't enough.

Vivienne crouched beside the vanity and pulled out a small tin of foundation powder. With practiced hands, she dulled her skin's porcelain glow, making it appear more uneven. She smudged her eyeliner, making her eyes seem tired and hollow. Then, for the final touch, she put on a worn baseball cap and tugged it low over her face.

She no longer looked like Vivienne Sinclair, the billionaire's bride-to-be.

She looked like nobody.

The hard part was next. Getting out.

She moved toward the large bay window, pressing her fingers against the cool glass. Outside, beyond the sprawling gardens of the Sinclair estate, security guards patrolled the perimeter. Their black suits and earpieces made them look more like agents from a secret intelligence agency rather than employees of a wedding.

Vivienne bit her lip. The front gate was impossible—too many eyes, too much attention. But the kitchen staff entrance at the back? That was a possibility.

Taking a steadying breath, she grabbed the duffel bag and pushed the window open just enough to squeeze through. A brisk wind swept through the room, carrying the scent of freshly cut grass and roses—her mother's favorite.

Her bare feet hit the ledge outside, and she lowered herself carefully onto the trellis below. The climb down was slow, her fingers gripping the wooden beams tightly as she descended. One wrong step, and she'd crash into the flower beds below—too much noise, too much risk.

Her heart thundered in her chest as she reached the ground.

The Perfect Wedding

Almost there.

She crouched low and darted toward the servants' pathway, keeping close to the hedges. Every shadow felt like a pair of watching eyes, every rustling leaf like the sound of a footstep behind her. She could hear the distant chatter of guests arriving, the hum of expensive cars pulling up to the estate.

Then—voices.

Vivienne flattened herself against the stone wall, gripping her bag tightly. Two security guards strolled past, laughing about something she couldn't quite hear. Her lungs burned from holding her breath.

They moved on.

This was it. Now or never.

She sprinted toward the back gate, reaching for the latch. It was unlocked. Relief flooded her, but she didn't have time to celebrate. She slipped through, her breath ragged as she ran down the service road leading away from the Sinclair estate.

The further she got, the lighter she felt. The mansion, the wedding, Ethan, her mother—all of it faded into the background.

She was free.

But freedom came with a price.

The Runaway Bride

Vivienne knew it wouldn't take long for someone to notice her absence. The security team would search the grounds, her mother would panic, Ethan would be furious. And when they found out she was truly gone, the media would explode.

A billionaire heiress vanishing on her wedding day? It would be everywhere.

But for now, she was just Elle—a girl running toward an uncertain future.

And for the first time in her life, that uncertainty felt exhilarating.

Two

Great Disappearance

Vivienne's lungs burned as she sprinted down the narrow back road, her legs aching from the sudden burst of exertion. The moon hung high above the vast estate, casting long shadows against the towering trees that lined the path. Crickets chirped in the distance, an eerie reminder of the stillness around her—stillness that wouldn't last for long.

Her hoodie flapped against her arms as she picked up speed, gripping the duffel bag against her side. She had no time to think, no time to hesitate. They would notice soon—if they hadn't already.

She glanced over her shoulder, her heart hammering.

The Sinclair estate still loomed behind her, its massive iron gates standing like a fortress against the outside world. The guards at the front likely had no idea she was gone yet, but that wouldn't last. If she wanted to disappear completely, she needed to be out of town before sunrise.

The road ahead was dimly lit by distant streetlights. It was a service road—one used by deliveries and staff, not guests. That meant fewer cars, fewer chances of being recognized.

Vivienne reached into her duffel bag, her fingers closing around the burner phone she had purchased weeks ago. Her real phone was still in her bridal suite, left intentionally on the nightstand as part of her cover. If they tracked her number, they would find nothing.

She tapped the screen. No signal.

Of course. She was still too close to the estate. She needed to get further away.

She swallowed down the rising panic and pressed forward, her sneakers slapping against the pavement. The road stretched ahead like an endless black river, leading into the unknown.

Just keep moving.

She had planned for this. She had rehearsed the escape over and over in her head, every step calculated. And yet, now that she was out in the open, it felt terrifyingly real.

A distant rumbling caught her attention.

Vivienne's head snapped up.

Headlights.

A car was approaching from the other end of the road, its beams cutting through the darkness. She cursed under her breath and dove into the tree line, crouching low behind a thick patch of bushes.

The vehicle slowed as it neared the estate, a sleek black sedan—the kind that belonged to security personnel.

Her pulse pounded in her ears as the car idled near the service gate. The driver's window rolled down.

Vivienne strained to hear.

"...Yeah, nothing yet," a man's voice muttered. "Bride's still inside, far as we know."

A second voice replied. "You sure? The boss is paranoid as hell. Told us to keep eyes everywhere tonight."

"I know. I know. We're doubling patrols." The first man sighed. "Harrington's got the guys on edge. He's convinced she's gonna bolt."

Vivienne clenched her jaw.

Ethan knew.

The Runaway Bride

Even before she had taken a step outside, he had suspected.

The car lingered for another moment before rolling forward, its tires crunching against the gravel. Vivienne stayed completely still, barely daring to breathe as the taillights disappeared around a bend.

Once the road was empty again, she pushed forward.

She followed the dirt path through the trees, her steps quieter now. She needed a ride—fast. But she couldn't risk hailing a cab from her usual accounts or even using her credit cards.

She needed cash only.

And she needed to get to the bus station before someone noticed she was gone.

She navigated through the wooded area until she reached the edge of town—a quieter side, where fewer people would recognize her. The streets were mostly deserted, the only movement coming from a few late-night stragglers.

A neon sign flickered ahead. 24-Hour Gas Station.

Vivienne pulled the baseball cap lower over her face and approached.

The station was mostly empty except for the bored-looking cashier behind the counter and a single customer—a trucker paying for his coffee.

Her gaze flicked to the side of the building. A public payphone.

Perfect.

She hurried toward it, gripping the cool metal receiver as she dropped a few quarters into the slot.

She dialed the only number she had memorized for this occasion.

The phone rang once.

Twice.

Then, a groggy voice answered.

"...Hello?"

Vivienne exhaled. "Marcus. It's me."

A pause. Then, sharp alertness. "Jesus, V. Do you have any idea how insane this is?"

"Not now. I need you to meet me."

"You ran?" He sounded equal parts exasperated and impressed. "Please tell me this isn't a joke."

"I don't have time for jokes, Marcus. Are you coming or not?"

A sigh. "Where are you?"

The Runaway Bride

She glanced around. "The gas station off Route 12."

"I can be there in twenty minutes."

"Make it fifteen."

The line went dead.

Vivienne hung up, her hands still trembling.

Marcus had been her only ally in this entire plan. A former Sinclair chauffeur who had left the job months ago, he was one of the few people she trusted. He knew how suffocating her life had been, and more importantly, he owed her a favor.

Fifteen minutes.

She could wait that long.

She stepped inside the gas station, grabbed a bottle of water, and kept her head down as she paid in cash. The cashier barely looked at her.

As she stepped back outside, she leaned against the cool brick wall, forcing herself to breathe.

Then—

A chirp from a police scanner.

Vivienne stiffened.

A squad car had pulled into the gas station.

Two officers. A man and a woman. They were talking to the cashier inside, pointing to a printed photo.

Her stomach dropped.

They were looking for her.

Her heart slammed against her ribs as she slowly edged around the corner of the building. She kept her movements casual, controlled. Running now would only draw attention.

She heard snippets of conversation.

"...Yes, missing since this evening..."

"...Possible sighting on surveillance..."

Her breath hitched.

They had her on camera.

Vivienne knew she had seconds—seconds—before they stepped back outside and spotted her.

She glanced toward the road. A pair of headlights turned the corner.

A familiar red pickup truck.

The Runaway Bride

Marcus.

Without thinking, she bolted toward it.

The moment she reached the door, Marcus threw it open. "Get in!"

Vivienne jumped in and slammed the door.

The officers turned, their gazes snapping toward the truck just as Marcus hit the gas.

Tires screeched as they sped away from the station.

Vivienne clutched the seat, her pulse racing.

Marcus glanced at her. "Hell of a wedding, huh?"

Vivienne let out a breathless, shaky laugh. "You have no idea."

Behind them, the flashing red and blue lights of a police car flicked on.

And the chase began.

Three

New Identity

The roar of the engine filled Vivienne's ears as Marcus gripped the wheel, his knuckles white as he floored the gas pedal. The red pickup truck shot forward, kicking up dust and gravel as they tore down the deserted highway.

Vivienne turned in her seat, her pulse a frantic drumbeat against her ribs. The police car was gaining on them, its red and blue lights flashing like a beacon in the night. Any second now, they'd flip on their siren. Any second now, she'd be caught.

This was not part of the plan.

"Marcus—"

"Hold on," he snapped, jerking the wheel hard to the right. The truck swerved onto an exit ramp, tires screeching as he took the curve too fast.

Vivienne's hands clenched the dashboard, bracing herself as the vehicle lurched forward. Behind them, the squad car hesitated at the turn, and for a moment, she thought they had lost them.

Then—

The sirens wailed.

"They're coming," she whispered.

Marcus didn't answer. His jaw was tight, his eyes locked onto the road ahead. The exit ramp led them to a quieter road, one lined with dark trees and a scattering of streetlights. It stretched into the distance like a black ribbon, offering nowhere to hide.

Vivienne's mind raced. She had planned for everything—cutting her hair, changing her clothes, ditching her real phone. But she hadn't planned for this. A car chase. The police on her tail.

She had to think. Fast.

"They're going to call for backup," she said, trying to steady her breathing. "If they do, roadblocks are next. We'll be trapped."

Marcus let out a humorless laugh. "You sure know how to pick your wedding nights."

New Identity

"Marcus."

He exhaled sharply. "There's a way out."

Vivienne snapped her gaze to him. "What?"

He nodded ahead. "There's a backroad coming up. Leads to the old industrial district—lots of abandoned warehouses, places to lay low. We take it, we might shake them."

She glanced over her shoulder. The squad car was still behind them, maybe a hundred yards back, pushing its engine to keep up.

Marcus pressed his foot down harder. The truck rumbled forward. The speedometer climbed—sixty, seventy, seventy-five. The trees blurred past.

The turn appeared up ahead, a barely noticeable gravel road, nearly swallowed by the darkness.

Marcus didn't slow down.

"Marcus—!"

At the last possible second, he wrenched the wheel to the right. The truck fishtailed as it veered off the highway, tires skidding across the gravel.

Vivienne slammed against the door, gasping as the vehicle bucked violently beneath them. The headlights barely illuminated the path ahead—an uneven, narrow road leading deeper into the industrial outskirts.

Behind them, the squad car barreled past the turn, missing it completely.

Vivienne sucked in a breath.

"They overshot!"

Marcus didn't slow down. "They'll double back," he warned. "We've got minutes, maybe less."

Vivienne scanned the area. The road was surrounded by abandoned lots, old factories with shattered windows, chain-link fences rusted with time.

"Where are we going?" she asked.

Marcus didn't answer. He swerved the truck off the path and into a narrow alley between two looming warehouse buildings. He killed the engine, plunging them into silence.

Vivienne's heartbeat thundered in her ears.

"Stay down," Marcus ordered, reaching over to kill the headlights.

Vivienne ducked low, pressing herself against the seat as she peered through the windshield.

New Identity

A moment later, the telltale flash of red and blue lights lit up the night sky.

The squad car had returned.

Her breath hitched.

The vehicle slowed as it reached the intersection, its headlights sweeping over the nearby buildings.

Marcus didn't move. Neither did she.

The silence was suffocating.

For a moment, it seemed like the officers might stop. They might get out. They might—

The squad car sped up, continuing down the road.

Vivienne waited, her entire body tense, until the lights disappeared completely.

Then—

Marcus exhaled.

"We're clear."

Vivienne let out a shaky breath, pressing a hand to her chest.

"That was too close," she whispered.

The Runaway Bride

Marcus leaned back in his seat, dragging a hand down his face. "You think?"

She turned to him. "We need to keep moving."

Marcus shook his head. "Not yet. We stay put until we're sure they aren't doubling back."

Vivienne clenched her fists. Every instinct screamed at her to run—to put as much distance between herself and the Sinclair estate as possible. But Marcus was right. Moving too soon could get them caught.

So she forced herself to sit still, to breathe, to listen.

The city around them was eerily quiet.

Finally, Marcus shifted. "Alright. Where to?"

Vivienne met his gaze.

"The train station."

Marcus frowned. "Not the bus station?"

"They'll expect the bus station. That's too obvious." She swallowed. "Trains have fewer cameras. Less security. If I can get out of the city by morning, I'll be harder to track."

Marcus was quiet for a moment, considering. Then he nodded. "Alright. Let's get you out of here."

New Identity

He started the truck again, this time keeping the headlights off as he maneuvered through the darkened streets.

Vivienne leaned her head back, exhaustion creeping in.

She had done it.

She had escaped the wedding. Escaped the estate.

But she wasn't free yet.

And she knew—deep down—that this was only the beginning.

—-

Three Hours Later – Train Station

Vivienne stepped onto the dimly lit platform, pulling her hoodie tighter around her.

Marcus stood beside her, arms crossed. "You sure about this?"

She nodded.

He sighed. "You got cash?"

She patted the duffel bag. "Enough to get by for a while."

He hesitated, then reached into his jacket, pulling out a small folded slip of paper. "Here. New ID. Fake, but it'll pass casual inspection."

Vivienne unfolded it. A driver's license.

Eleanor 'Elle' Monroe.

She traced the name with her thumb. It felt strange. Unfamiliar.

But it was hers now.

"Elle," she murmured.

Marcus shifted awkwardly. "It's not much, but it'll keep you hidden."

Vivienne—Elle—looked up at him. "Thank you, Marcus. For everything."

He rubbed the back of his neck. "You gonna be okay?"

"I'll figure it out."

He nodded, though he still looked unconvinced. "Train leaves in five. Better go."

Elle hesitated for only a second. Then she turned away, stepping onto the platform.

She didn't look back.

The train doors hissed open, and she stepped inside.

As she found a seat and settled in, the realization hit her.

New Identity

Vivienne Sinclair was gone.

Elle Monroe had taken her place.

And whatever happened next—

She was on her own.

Four

Meeting the Writer

The train rattled along the tracks, a low hum vibrating through the floor beneath Elle's feet. The air inside the cabin was heavy with the scent of old leather seats, metal, and the faint remnants of someone's cheap cologne. A few passengers sat scattered throughout, their faces obscured by fatigue, indifference, or the glow of their phone screens.

Elle kept her baseball cap pulled low, her hood raised slightly to shadow her face. Every time the train slowed, her muscles tensed, waiting for the inevitable—officers boarding the train, searching for a missing billionaire bride.

But no one came.

The train was an old commuter line, not the kind that security officers frequently patrolled. The anonymity of the journey comforted her, but only slightly. She wasn't safe. Not yet.

The rhythmic clatter of the wheels against the tracks filled the silence as she exhaled slowly, trying to calm herself down.

She was Elle Monroe now. Not Vivienne Sinclair.

Vivienne belonged to another world—the world of gilded cages, suffocating expectations, and ruthless billionaires.

Elle Monroe was a ghost. A runaway. A woman with no past and no ties.

And ghosts didn't get caught.

Her fingers tightened around the strap of her duffel bag as the train lurched, slowing as it pulled into a new station. She shifted slightly in her seat, resisting the urge to look outside. This was a stop in one of the smaller towns along the line—a place where no one would be looking for her.

She could disappear here.

She would disappear here.

The doors hissed open, and a handful of passengers stepped on.

Among them was a man.

He was tall, lean, and a little disheveled, carrying a worn

leather messenger bag slung over his shoulder. Dark brown curls fell messily over his forehead, and his eyes—intense and shadowed with fatigue—swept over the train cabin with the quick precision of someone who noticed everything.

Elle stilled.

Something about him—his presence, his energy—set her on edge. He didn't belong here, not in the way the other tired travelers did.

She pulled her hood lower, keeping her gaze down as he walked past her row and dropped into the seat directly across from her.

Her heart kicked up a notch.

Of all the empty seats, he had to sit there?

She forced herself to stay still, to breathe normally, even as he shifted in his seat, adjusting his bag. A moment later, he let out a sigh and pulled out a notebook, flipping it open with practiced ease.

A pen appeared in his fingers, tapping absently against the lined pages before he began to write.

Elle frowned slightly.

He wasn't watching her. He wasn't paying her any attention at all.

Still, she remained wary.

The minutes stretched on, filled only by the faint scratching of his pen against paper.

Her curiosity got the better of her.

She stole a glance.

The man was writing furiously, his brows furrowed in deep concentration. Whatever he was working on, he was lost in it, oblivious to everything else around him.

She exhaled slowly, her shoulders relaxing slightly.

Not a threat.

Just... a writer.

Another stop passed, and the train continued its journey. The man kept writing, occasionally pausing to cross something out before jotting down something new.

Elle tried not to pay attention. She really did.

But then—

A frustrated groan.

She glanced up in time to see him slam his pen down and run a hand through his already messy curls.

"Damn it," he muttered under his breath.

Elle blinked.

Without meaning to, she spoke.

"Writer's block?"

The man looked up sharply, his dark eyes locking onto hers. For a moment, he seemed surprised she had spoken at all. Then, a wry smirk tugged at his lips.

"You could say that," he admitted, leaning back against the seat. "Or just a complete lack of talent. Hard to tell which at this point."

Elle arched a brow. "That bad?"

He exhaled, rubbing the back of his neck. "Let's just say if I had a dollar for every draft I've thrown away, I wouldn't be on this train—I'd be on a private jet, living on an island somewhere."

Something about the casual way he spoke unnerved her.

He had no idea that she actually knew what that world was like. The world of private jets and island vacations, of wealth and excess.

The world she had just escaped from.

"You're a writer?" she asked, carefully keeping her tone neutral.

"That's what I tell myself to justify my terrible life choices," he said, smirking. Then, he seemed to study her, as if realizing for the first time that she wasn't just another exhausted traveler.

"You don't look like the usual crowd on this train," he observed.

Elle stiffened slightly. "Neither do you."

His smirk widened. "Fair enough."

A beat of silence passed. Then, he tilted his head. "What's your name?"

A simple question. An innocent one.

But it sent a spike of panic through her.

Her instinct was to lie.

But she had prepared for this.

She had a name. A new identity.

She forced herself to relax, offering a small, careful smile.

"Elle," she said. "Elle Monroe."

The name tasted strange in her mouth, but she kept her expression unreadable.

The man studied her for a second longer before nodding.

"Noah," he said, offering his hand. "Noah Carter."

She hesitated, then shook it. His grip was warm, firm—but not overbearing.

"So, Elle Monroe," he said, leaning back in his seat. "What's your story?"

Her pulse quickened.

She kept her fingers wrapped around the strap of her duffel bag, her mind racing.

She needed to be careful.

She wasn't Vivienne Sinclair anymore.

Elle Monroe was just a regular girl.

She had to make him believe that.

"Not much of a story," she said, keeping her tone light. "Just needed a change of scenery."

Noah arched a brow. "Running from something?"

Her throat went dry.

But before she could answer, the train's intercom crackled to life.

Meeting the Writer

"Next stop: Willow Springs. Arriving in ten minutes."

Relief flooded her.

She had made it.

No more trains. No more near-misses.

This was where she would start over.

Noah stretched, stuffing his notebook back into his bag. "Well, Elle Monroe, looks like this is my stop too."

She froze.

"What?"

He shot her a grin. "I live in Willow Springs."

Elle's stomach twisted.

What were the chances?

She was supposed to disappear, to blend into the background.

But now, she had just crossed paths with someone who might be impossible to ignore.

And for the first time, she wondered—

Had she just made a mistake?

Five

Normal Life

The train came to a slow, grinding halt at the Willow Springs station, the hiss of the brakes breaking through the low murmur of the passengers inside. Elle's pulse quickened as she gripped the strap of her duffel bag, forcing herself to keep her movements casual. She had made it. She had escaped. But this was the real challenge—blending in, surviving as Elle Monroe, a girl with no past and no ties.

And yet, as she rose to her feet, slinging the bag over her shoulder, she was keenly aware of one problem she hadn't anticipated.

Noah Carter was getting off at the same stop.

She still wasn't sure what to make of him. Their conversation on the train had been too easy, too natural. He had an air of confidence, the kind that suggested he didn't believe in coincidences. And that made her uneasy.

She adjusted her baseball cap, tugging it lower over her face as she stepped onto the platform. The cool night air brushed against her skin, carrying the faint scent of rain-soaked pavement and distant pine trees. Willow Springs was smaller than she had expected—just a modest little town nestled between mountains and rivers, far away from the world she had left behind.

She could disappear here.

At least, that was the plan.

But now Noah was walking beside her, matching her pace with an ease that made her feel like she was already being watched.

"So," he said, stuffing his hands into his jacket pockets. "You got a place to stay, Elle Monroe?"

Her fingers tensed around her duffel bag.

She hadn't expected that question, at least not this soon.

"I'll figure it out," she said smoothly, hoping the conversation would end there.

Noah let out a short laugh. "You don't sound too sure about that."

Elle glanced at him from under the brim of her cap. "I'm sure enough."

She could feel him studying her.

"Right," he said slowly. "So you just picked Willow Springs at random? Decided this was as good a place as any to start over?"

Her breath caught. Too close. Too perceptive.

"I like small towns," she said simply.

It wasn't a lie. It was just a convenient truth.

Noah didn't press further. Instead, he nodded toward the only open coffee shop across the street, the neon sign flickering dimly.

"Tell you what," he said. "I owe you one."

She blinked. "For what?"

"For distracting me on the train. Kept me from setting my own notebook on fire."

His tone was light, teasing. But Elle knew better. Nothing was ever that simple.

"I don't need a favor," she said carefully.

"Good, because I wasn't offering one." He gestured toward the coffee shop. "But if you're planning on figuring things out, might as well start with a cup of coffee."

Elle hesitated.

It was dangerous to let anyone in. Even a little.

But she had no idea where to go next. No clue where she was supposed to sleep tonight, no contacts, no backup plan beyond not getting caught.

One cup of coffee wouldn't kill her.

Right?

She exhaled slowly. "Fine."

Noah grinned, as if he had expected her to say yes. "Come on, then."

Inside the Coffee Shop

The small diner-style café smelled of fresh coffee and baked goods, the warmth immediately wrapping around her like a cocoon. The walls were lined with old bookshelves filled with secondhand novels, and a chalkboard menu hung over the counter, the letters slightly smudged from too many changes.

Elle followed Noah to a booth in the back, making sure to sit with her back to the wall.

Noah, of course, noticed.

"Paranoid much?" he asked, smirking.

She lifted a brow. "Cautious."

He chuckled, flagging down the waitress. She was older, maybe in her fifties, with graying hair tied up in a messy bun.

"Two coffees, please," Noah said.

The waitress scribbled on her notepad, then glanced at Elle. "You new around here?"

Elle tensed slightly.

Noah, ever observant, answered before she could. "She's just passing through."

Elle shot him a look, but he just shrugged.

The waitress hummed. "Well, welcome to Willow Springs, sweetheart. Not much happens around here, but it's a nice place."

Elle forced a polite smile. "Thanks."

As soon as the waitress left, Noah leaned forward, resting his elbows on the table. "So," he said. "What's your deal?"

She frowned. "Excuse me?"

"Your deal. You show up on a late-night train, no luggage except a duffel bag, no real explanation as to why you're here, and you have the instincts of someone who's hiding from something."

Elle's heart skipped a beat.

Noah watched her reaction carefully, but she schooled her features into a neutral expression.

"That's a lot of assumptions," she said coolly.

He tilted his head. "Am I wrong?"

Elle didn't blink. "I just needed a change. That's all."

Noah leaned back, studying her. "Fair enough."

The waitress returned, setting two steaming mugs of coffee on the table before disappearing again. Elle wrapped her hands around hers, letting the warmth seep into her fingers.

"Look," Noah said after a moment. "I don't know what you're running from, and I won't ask. But if you're planning to stick around here, you're gonna need a job."

Elle glanced at him warily. "And you just happen to have one?"

He smirked. "Not me. But Margaret might."

"Margaret?"

"The old lady who runs the bookstore down the street. She's always looking for help."

Elle's fingers tightened slightly around her mug.

A bookstore.

That... could work. It was quiet, out of the way. No high-profile customers, no reason for the media to come sniffing around.

Noah noticed her hesitation. "It's that or sleeping in the train station."

Elle sighed, taking a sip of her coffee. It was bitter, but in a way that felt grounding.

"Fine," she said after a moment.

Noah grinned. "Good choice."

The Walk to the Bookstore

The night air was crisp as they left the café, the streets quiet except for the occasional passing car. Elle kept her hands tucked into her hoodie pockets, walking beside Noah in silence.

The bookstore was just up ahead—a quaint, old-fashioned shop with a wooden sign that read 'Foster's Books'. The windows were dark, but a single light glowed inside.

Noah stopped in front of the door, tapping on the glass.

After a moment, the lock clicked, and the door swung open to reveal Margaret Foster.

She was older, with silver hair pinned into a loose bun and sharp blue eyes that immediately took in everything about Elle—her worn hoodie, her tired eyes, the duffel bag slung over her shoulder.

Noah grinned. "Margaret, meet Elle. She needs a job."

Margaret arched a brow, crossing her arms. "Is that so?"

Elle met her gaze evenly.

"Yes."

Margaret studied her for a long moment.

Then, with a small nod, she stepped aside.

"Come in."

Elle exhaled, stepping over the threshold.

And just like that, she had taken the first step into her new life.

Six

First Spark

The small brass bell over the door jingled softly as Elle stepped into Foster's Books. The scent of old paper and leather bindings enveloped her immediately, grounding her in something familiar yet completely foreign at the same time. The shop was dimly lit, with warm yellow lamps casting long shadows over tall wooden bookshelves that stretched nearly to the ceiling.

It was cozy, quiet—exactly the kind of place where a runaway billionaire bride could disappear.

Margaret Foster shut the door behind them, flipping the sign to Closed before turning to study Elle properly. The older woman was sharp-eyed, with deep-set wrinkles and an air of no-nonsense practicality. She wore a dark cardigan over a long skirt, her gray hair pulled into a loose bun, wisps escaping around her face.

She crossed her arms. "So, you need a job."

Elle met her gaze evenly. "Yes."

Margaret glanced at Noah, arching a brow. "And you're vouching for her?"

Noah smirked. "She's got that lost puppy look. Thought I'd bring her to you before she ended up sleeping in the train station."

Elle bristled but bit her tongue. She was not a lost puppy.

Margaret sighed. "You do realize I can't just hire someone off the street with no references, right?"

Elle swallowed. She had expected that. Normal people had resumes, past job experiences, something to vouch for their reliability. She had none of that.

But she had to try.

"I can work hard," she said quickly. "I know books. I can organize, manage stock, help customers. Whatever you need."

Margaret's eyes narrowed slightly. "You sound desperate."

Elle was desperate.

Before she could answer, Noah leaned casually against the counter. "Come on, Margaret. You always say you need help around here. And look at her—she won't steal from you. She's clearly on the run from something."

Elle shot him a sharp look, but Margaret just let out a dry laugh.

"Oh, I know that," the older woman said, surprising Elle. She turned back, fixing her with a piercing stare. "The real question is—are you running from trouble, or are you bringing trouble here?"

Elle's mouth went dry.

Margaret Foster wasn't a fool.

The bookstore owner held her gaze, waiting.

For a brief moment, Elle considered lying. Saying she was just traveling, that she had lost her job, that she was just starting over.

But something about Margaret's expression told her it wouldn't work.

So instead, she chose her words carefully.

"I just needed to get away," she said, her voice quieter now. "From a life that didn't fit me anymore."

Margaret studied her for a long moment.

Then, she exhaled. "Fine."

Elle blinked. "Fine?"

"You can start tomorrow," Margaret said, already walking toward the back room. "Opening shift is at eight. Don't be late."

Elle's breath caught in her throat. That was it?

Noah grinned, nudging her shoulder. "Told you she was a softie."

Margaret shot him a glare. "Don't push your luck, Carter."

Elle didn't know what to say. She had expected resistance. She had expected to be turned away.

But instead—she had a job. A place to hide.

Maybe even a place to belong.

—-

Later That Night – The Guest Room

Elle sat on the edge of the small bed in the tiny upstairs room above Foster's Books, her duffel bag at her feet. Margaret had offered her the space without hesitation, telling her it was used for storage but that it had a cot and a bathroom.

The Runaway Bride

It was small, but it was safe.

Safe enough.

She pulled off her baseball cap, running a hand through her short hair. It still felt strange, feeling how short it was, the way the strands barely brushed her shoulders.

She wasn't Vivienne Sinclair anymore.

She had really done it.

She had walked away from everything.

A life of wealth, luxury, a future set in stone—she had left it all behind.

She should have felt relief.

But instead, she felt something else.

Anxiety.

Her family would be searching for her. The news would be everywhere by now. There would be reporters, speculation, theories.

Ethan Harrington would be furious.

She closed her eyes, breathing slowly.

First Spark

She had to be careful. She couldn't let her guard down.

This was only the beginning.

—-

The Next Day – First Day on the Job

Elle's hands hovered over the stack of books, carefully aligning the spines before placing them on the shelf. The bookstore had been open for an hour, and so far, it had been… peaceful.

Margaret worked at the register, greeting the few early-morning customers, while Elle focused on restocking and organizing.

It was so different from the world she had left behind.

No assistants. No security guards. No extravagant events.

Just books, the soft sound of pages turning, and the scent of fresh coffee from the small café attached to the shop.

She liked it.

Or at least—she wanted to.

She had just finished organizing a display when the bell over the door jingled.

Elle looked up.

The Runaway Bride

Noah Carter strolled in, looking annoyingly comfortable, as if he owned the place.

"You again?" Elle muttered.

Noah grinned. "You sound thrilled to see me."

Margaret barely looked up. "If you're just here to bother my new employee, Carter, I'll throw you out myself."

Noah held up his hands in mock surrender. "I actually came for coffee."

Elle rolled her eyes, returning to her task.

She was shelving a book when she felt Noah's presence beside her.

"So," he said, leaning against the shelf. "How's the first day?"

She hesitated, then shrugged. "It's... quiet."

"That's a good thing, right?"

She nodded. "Yeah. It is."

Noah watched her for a moment. Then, his smirk faded slightly.

"You know," he said, "you're really bad at pretending to be just another girl passing through."

First Spark

Elle's grip on the book tightened.

She turned her head slightly, her green eyes locking onto his. "What's that supposed to mean?"

Noah tilted his head. "It means I've met a lot of people who are running from something. And you?" He paused. "You don't look like someone who's used to running. You look like someone who's used to being chased."

A sharp jolt of panic shot through her chest.

For a second, she forgot how to breathe.

He knew.

Or at least—he suspected.

But Noah didn't push further. Instead, he grabbed a book off the shelf, flipping it open casually.

"Relax," he said. "I don't care who you are."

Elle exhaled slowly. "Good."

"But," he added, flashing her a grin, "I do care if you make good coffee. Because if you screw up my order, we're gonna have a problem."

Elle rolled her eyes.

But deep down—deep, deep down—she knew.

Noah Carter wasn't just another stranger in town.

And something about him was going to be a problem.

She just didn't know how big of a problem yet.

Seven

Secrets and Stories

Elle sat in the corner of Foster's Books, the hum of the overhead lights above her head. The morning rush had died down, leaving her alone with the bookshelves and the quiet murmur of Margaret's voice as she spoke to a regular customer in the front of the store. Elle had spent the better part of the morning reorganizing the fiction section, moving books from one shelf to another, ensuring that everything was perfectly aligned. The task had helped her focus, helped to keep her mind from wandering into dangerous territory.

She had worked for hours without distraction, and for the first time in a long while, she found a small measure of peace in the rhythm of her work. But then—the bell over the door chimed again, and her stomach lurched.

Noah.

The Runaway Bride

He strolled in casually, hands stuffed into his pockets, eyes scanning the store like it was his second home. The warm smell of coffee clung to him—he must've stopped by the café. He was probably here just to grab a drink and leave.

But then, he looked at her. His eyes met hers with a knowing glance, his lips curling into a grin that wasn't quite friendly, but more... inquisitive.

Elle swallowed, her fingers still gripping the spine of the book she was holding. He was getting harder to ignore.

"I'll never get used to the smell of books," Noah said, his voice pulling her from her thoughts. He stepped closer, his gaze flicking to the shelves before returning to her.

She resisted the urge to roll her eyes. "You've been in here, what, three times this week?"

"I'm a man of habit," he said with a shrug. "I like things I can rely on. And coffee and books are reliable. So here I am, again."

Elle forced a tight smile. "Right."

He didn't leave. Instead, he took a seat at the nearby table, his eyes fixed on her as he propped up his feet on the chair in front of him. It wasn't the first time Noah had stayed longer than necessary. He had a way of lingering—of watching. It made her nervous, but she couldn't put her finger on why.

"Don't you have work to do?" she asked, trying to break the

tension, though she knew it was futile. Noah never seemed like he had any particular purpose, always showing up at odd times without explanation.

"I do," he said, not missing a beat. "But I'm in no rush."

Elle couldn't help herself. She glanced at him, her curiosity tugging at her. "So, what exactly do you do?"

Noah's eyes glinted with amusement. "Do you always ask that many questions?"

Her cheeks flushed slightly. "I'm just curious."

He studied her for a long moment, his face unreadable. Finally, he leaned back in his chair, stretching his legs out in front of him. "I'm a writer," he said, letting the words linger in the air between them. "You know—books, stories, the usual."

Elle's heart skipped.

A writer.

The thought of it suddenly made everything about him seem a little too... familiar. The way he observed people, the way he made people feel like they were under a microscope.

"Is that so?" she asked, her voice low.

Noah tilted his head, studying her with curiosity. "You sound surprised."

The Runaway Bride

Elle hesitated. Her first instinct was to back away, to change the subject, to pretend she didn't care. She had no business getting involved with him. But something about his presence made it impossible to keep up the distance.

"Maybe I didn't expect it," she said, forcing herself to meet his eyes. "Why do you write?"

His expression softened slightly, and for a brief moment, Elle saw something genuine in his gaze—a flicker of vulnerability. But it was gone as quickly as it had appeared.

"Because it's the only way I can make sense of this place," Noah said quietly, his voice taking on an edge of rawness that made Elle's breath catch. "This whole world. You'd be surprised how much you can understand about people when you write them down."

Elle's pulse quickened. It was as though his words were too close, like he had peeked into a part of her life she had buried deep inside. She couldn't help herself—she leaned in slightly.

"People?" she asked, her voice barely a whisper.

He nodded, a small smile tugging at his lips. "Characters, really. The ones you meet, the ones you don't. Sometimes I wonder if everyone's a character in someone else's story, you know?"

Elle swallowed, suddenly feeling a chill despite the warmth in the room. "You're talking about fiction?"

Noah's gaze never left hers, his eyes intense. "Of course. But isn't all life just a little bit of fiction, too? We tell ourselves stories to survive. It's how we get by. How we make sense of the chaos."

Elle's mind spun.

She had spent her whole life living in a carefully constructed narrative. She had been Vivienne Sinclair, the perfect heiress, the perfect bride-to-be, destined for a life of luxury and privilege. That story had been written for her. It wasn't until she ran away that she realized how false it all was.

And now here she was—living a life that felt more like a dream than reality, caught somewhere between who she had been and who she was trying to become.

"Are you writing my story, then?" Elle asked, unable to stop herself.

Noah's expression flickered. "I think I'm still trying to figure out if you're real."

The words hung in the air like an unspoken challenge. Elle's heart pounded in her chest, a flutter of anxiety mixed with something else—a strange sense of being seen.

Before she could respond, the sound of the shop door opening made them both turn. Margaret stepped in from the back room, glancing between the two of them.

"Am I interrupting something?" she asked, her voice sharp and to the point.

Elle quickly composed herself, straightening up and stepping away from the table. "No, not at all."

Margaret eyed them both, then fixed her gaze on Noah. "You're still here, Carter?"

Noah flashed a grin. "I swear I'm not stalking her."

Margaret snorted, clearly not buying it. "If you say so. Just don't get in the way of the business, alright?"

Noah raised his hands in mock surrender. "I'll leave when I'm ready, don't worry."

Margaret rolled her eyes and turned back to Elle. "We're closing in about an hour. I'll need you to lock up."

"Sure," Elle replied, a tightness in her chest she couldn't shake.

As Margaret walked to the back again, Elle's mind raced.

What was Noah playing at? Why had he been so insistent on talking to her? And why did his words keep gnawing at her, like they were stirring something inside her she couldn't put into words?

She tried to push the thoughts away as Noah stood up, stretching and glancing at the door. "I should get going. Got more work to do. But hey," he said, his voice lowering slightly. "I'll be back tomorrow. You don't get off that easy."

Elle blinked. "What do you mean?"

He smiled again, but it wasn't as playful as before. It was almost... knowing. "You'll see."

With that, he turned and walked out of the store, the bell jingling softly behind him.

Elle stood there for a long moment, her heart pounding in her chest.

Something was off.

Noah Carter wasn't just another small-town writer. He was more than that. She could feel it.

And the more he lingered around her, the harder it became to pretend she wasn't afraid of the secrets he was starting to unravel.

Eight

Hidden Truth

The bell above the door chimed again, pulling Elle from her thoughts. She had been staring at the books in front of her, lost in a haze of uncertainty. The words Noah had spoken to her the day before—the ones about writing people's stories—had gnawed at her all night. He hadn't just been asking questions. He had been observing her.

She could feel it now, the weight of his presence, the way he seemed to see through her with just a glance. Every time he walked into the bookstore, every time his eyes locked with hers, it felt like he was pulling her into a different reality—a reality where nothing about her was safe.

She shook her head, trying to dispel the thoughts, but they were persistent. He's just a guy. That's all he was. She was overthinking it.

The door jingled again, and she lifted her gaze.

It wasn't Noah.

A man had entered, tall and broad-shouldered, dressed in a dark coat and a baseball cap that shadowed his face. His eyes scanned the bookstore briefly before settling on Elle, and the second their gazes met, something in his expression changed. He tilted his head slightly, as if recognizing her.

Elle's breath caught. She wasn't used to being recognized, and the feeling left a bitter taste in her mouth.

The man took a few slow steps toward her, his eyes fixed on her face. He seemed to study her carefully, and for a moment, the world around her went silent.

It took her a moment to realize she was holding her breath. She straightened up, feeling the tension coil in her chest. Don't panic. Don't make it obvious.

"Excuse me," the man said, his voice low and calm, but with an edge of curiosity. "You're the woman from the news, aren't you?"

Elle's stomach dropped. Her heart hammered in her chest.

No one had approached her like this before. She had successfully stayed under the radar, had disappeared. But this man—he had seen her. He had recognized her.

The Runaway Bride

"I'm sorry, I think you have me confused with someone else," Elle said, forcing a casual tone, even as her mind raced. She had to act normal. If she gave anything away, it would be over.

The man didn't move, his eyes never leaving hers. "No," he said quietly, his voice sharp. "You're Vivienne Sinclair, aren't you?"

The name hit her like a punch to the gut. Her old identity, the one she had fought so hard to escape, was alive again, out there, following her. She could feel her throat go dry. This was not happening.

"I don't know what you're talking about," Elle replied, her voice faltering slightly. She stepped back, her pulse racing.

The man smiled—a small, almost sad smile, as if he knew she was lying.

"I don't blame you for hiding," he said, his voice oddly kind. "I know what it's like to want to disappear."

Elle's breath caught. He wasn't threatening her. But the words—those words—they felt like a trap.

"Who are you?" Elle demanded, her voice steadier than she felt.

The man's smile faltered, and he glanced toward the door as if making sure no one was watching. He then lowered his voice and took a step closer. "I'm not here to hurt you," he said, his tone genuine. "I'm here to help."

Elle's mind spun. Help? Why would anyone want to help her? She was supposed to be invisible, not targeted for help.

"Help?" she repeated, trying to mask the unease in her voice. "How exactly do you think you can help me?"

The man's eyes softened, and he took another step toward her, lowering his voice further. "I'm a private investigator. I've been hired to find you, Vivienne."

The word private investigator echoed in her ears like a death sentence. This was it. The moment her old life had finally caught up to her. She had known it was inevitable—they would find her eventually. But now, standing before her was proof. The name. The job. The hunt.

Her throat tightened.

"I'm not Vivienne Sinclair," Elle said firmly, this time with more authority. She lifted her chin, forcing herself to look him straight in the eye. "I'm Elle Monroe."

The man didn't seem convinced, but he didn't press the issue immediately. Instead, he held her gaze, his expression unreadable.

"You're a good liar," he said finally. "I'll give you that."

She felt a wave of panic rise within her. It was obvious now that he wasn't fooled. He wasn't going to let her slip away so easily.

"Look," the man continued, his voice still low. "I'm not here to expose you. I'm just trying to find out what happened. Why you disappeared."

Elle's breath hitched. The truth of what she had done—what she had become—felt like it was pushing up through her throat. She could tell this man was trying to get under her skin, trying to dig for something he could use.

"Who hired you?" she demanded, trying to control the situation. She didn't want to show him any weakness, but it was hard when her past was being dragged out like this.

"I'm not at liberty to say," he replied cryptically, his eyes never leaving hers. "But what I can tell you is this—I know about your fiancé. Ethan Harrington."

Elle flinched, the name cutting through her like a knife. She had hoped that maybe, just maybe, he wouldn't be part of this equation. But of course, he was. He would always be part of her story, even if she never wanted it.

"Ethan's not looking for me anymore," she said quickly, too quickly. "He knows where I am. I've—moved on."

The man's gaze darkened. "You think he's just going to let you go like that? The Sinclair name carries weight, even when you try to run from it. Ethan might be pretending to let you go, but he's got a bounty on your head, Vivienne. He's been searching for you ever since you vanished. And he won't stop until he finds you."

Elle's chest tightened, and for the first time since she'd left, she felt the real weight of the lie she had been living. It wasn't just about escaping the wedding or escaping Ethan—it was about eluding a life that would never let her go.

"I don't want any part of that life anymore," Elle said, her voice trembling slightly. "I'm not Vivienne Sinclair. I'm Elle Monroe. And I'm not going back."

The man tilted his head, his gaze sharpening. "You don't get to choose that. Once you're in the Sinclair world, it doesn't let you go. It pulls you back. Whether you want it or not."

His words hit her like a cold slap.

"I can't keep running," Elle said, her voice almost a whisper. "I've done everything I could to escape. I just want to be left alone."

The man's eyes softened for a moment, as though he almost understood. But then, he shook his head. "I'm not here to make you go back. I'm here to warn you. You think you're safe, but you're not. Ethan will find you. And when he does, there's no telling what he'll do to get you back."

Elle swallowed, the fear she'd been pushing down rising up to take over. "What do you want from me?"

"I want you to understand what you're up against," the man said, his voice steady. "You don't get to just disappear. You have to fight for your freedom."

Elle's mind raced. She had no idea what kind of world she had just walked back into. The life she had tried to escape was not done with her. It would never let her go.

The man turned to leave but paused by the door. "I'll be watching, Vivienne," he said quietly. "You can't hide forever."

The door clicked shut behind him, and the bookstore went eerily silent.

Elle stood frozen in place, her thoughts swirling in a storm of fear and confusion.

She had no idea what to do next.

But she knew one thing for certain: her past was closing in, and there was no way to outrun it.

Nine

Investigator's Shadow

Elle stood frozen for a long moment, staring at the door through which the man had just disappeared. The hum of the overhead lights in the bookstore seemed louder now, almost suffocating. The words he had spoken echoed in her mind, his voice a constant undercurrent of threat and warning.

"You can't hide forever."

Her hands were trembling, and she forced them into the pockets of her hoodie, trying to steady herself. The weight of his gaze, the cold certainty in his voice—it was like he had seen through every single lie she had constructed, every attempt to hide her past.

She didn't know what to do. Ethan—the man who had

once claimed to love her, the man who had demanded her compliance in everything—wasn't just going to let her vanish. He was out there, somewhere, and he would come for her.

Elle squeezed her eyes shut, trying to block out the crushing reality of it all. It was too much, too overwhelming. She had run, yes, but had she really escaped? Had she ever truly been free?

"Elle?"

Margaret's voice, sharp and direct, broke through the haze of her thoughts. Elle turned to find the older woman standing just inside the back room, her arms crossed. Margaret's eyes held a mixture of curiosity and suspicion, as though she had been watching from afar and waiting for the right moment to intervene.

"You alright?"

Elle swallowed hard, trying to hide the panic that was threatening to overtake her. "Yeah," she said, her voice a little too high-pitched. "Just... just needed a moment."

Margaret raised an eyebrow, clearly unconvinced, but she didn't press. Instead, she nodded toward the counter. "You've been working hard all day. Why don't you take a break? I'll watch the shop for a bit."

"Thanks," Elle said, managing a small smile, though it felt forced. She needed a moment—just a few minutes to herself. She didn't

Investigator's Shadow

want Margaret asking any more questions, not when her mind was spinning.

As Elle made her way toward the back of the store, she passed the window overlooking the street. Her breath caught in her throat when she noticed a black SUV parked across the street.

A chill washed over her. The tinted windows obscured the driver, but the vehicle was positioned in a way that made it impossible not to see the bookstore. It was watching her.

She hurried into the back room, away from the window, her pulse thudding in her ears. There was a strange, sinking feeling in her stomach—a feeling of being trapped. Had the investigator followed her here? Was he really going to keep shadowing her every move until she broke?

She leaned against the door, her back pressed to the wood, and tried to calm her racing thoughts.

There had to be something she could do. Some way out of this. No one was going to take her back to that life.

She was Elle Monroe now. Not Vivienne Sinclair.

Yet, the more she tried to convince herself, the more the dread settled in. How long could she keep running? How long until the walls of her new life closed in?

The door opened behind her, and Elle straightened up, wiping her palms on her jeans. Margaret stood there, her eyes fixed on her.

"You've been looking out the window for a while," she said, her tone laced with concern. "Is something going on out there?"

Elle's heart skipped a beat. She tried to control the panic bubbling in her chest. "I'm fine," she said, her voice hoarse. "Just... just thinking."

Margaret didn't seem convinced, but she didn't press. "Alright. But you've been acting a bit strange today. Is everything okay?"

Elle hesitated. The investigator was still out there, in that SUV, watching her every move. Her skin tingled with the weight of his scrutiny. She couldn't tell Margaret the truth. She couldn't risk it.

"I just need to focus," Elle said, forcing herself to sound confident. "I can handle it. Don't worry about me."

Margaret's sharp eyes lingered for a moment longer before she nodded, though Elle could see the doubt still etched on her face. "Well, don't stay locked away for too long. The customers will be coming in soon."

Elle managed a tight smile. "Of course."

Margaret left her alone again, and Elle's mind immediately returned to the SUV outside. Her hand instinctively went to the window, peering through the blinds. The SUV was still parked there, the engine off, but the figure inside was still concealed by the darkness of the tinted windows.

She was being watched.

Elle felt a rush of panic, and the desire to run surged through her veins. But where would she go? The town was small, the streets familiar to the locals—and if the investigator was watching her, she was certain that every corner was now a potential trap.

The sound of the bell above the door broke her concentration. Elle pulled away from the window and quickly composed herself, trying to act like everything was normal. But when she stepped back into the store, her eyes immediately darted to the front door.

The man—the investigator—was standing in the doorway. His posture was relaxed, but his eyes were sharp, scanning the room as he stepped inside. He was wearing a dark coat and a baseball cap, much like before, but there was something in the way he moved now—more confident, more deliberate.

Elle's breath caught in her throat. She couldn't escape him. He had found her again.

"Hello, Margaret," the investigator said smoothly, his voice smooth and polite. "Just thought I'd stop by for a quick visit."

Margaret didn't seem surprised, though she eyed him carefully. "Can I help you with something?"

"Just browsing," he said with a casual smile, his gaze flicking to

Elle. She felt a chill shoot up her spine.

The investigator stepped further into the store, taking a slow walk toward the bookshelves. His eyes never fully left Elle, and it was clear he was trying to gauge her reaction.

Margaret's eyes narrowed, but she didn't say anything. She went back to her work, though Elle could see the tension in her shoulders.

The investigator walked past her, his hand trailing over the spines of the books. Every step felt like it was an eternity. Elle didn't know what to do, how to act. Should she confront him? Or should she stay quiet and hope he would leave?

He stopped in front of a shelf and pulled out a book, flipping through it absentmindedly. He was clearly biding his time, watching her without looking too obvious.

For a brief moment, Elle considered running—leaving. But where would she go? She couldn't just disappear again.

Then, the investigator spoke again. "You know, Margaret," he said, his voice too casual. "I've been trying to figure out where Elle Monroe came from. It's a pretty common name, don't you think? How is it that she ended up here, in this little town, all by herself?"

Margaret stiffened, her back to him as she continued working. She said nothing.

Elle's stomach twisted in a way that made her want to scream. He wasn't being subtle anymore. He had connected the dots. He was testing her—pushing her, seeing if she would crack.

"I think," he continued, turning to face her, "you might know more than you're letting on."

Elle's blood ran cold, but she refused to show it. She met his gaze head-on. "I don't know what you're talking about."

The investigator smiled, but it wasn't a friendly smile. It was calculating, dangerous. "I think you do, Elle," he said softly. "I really do."

For a moment, the world seemed to pause. Elle felt like the walls were closing in. He was so close. Too close. She couldn't keep running. She had no idea how much longer she could hold out.

But then, he turned and walked toward the door. "I'll be seeing you again soon," he called over his shoulder. "Don't worry, I won't be far behind."

The door closed softly behind him.

Elle was left standing in the middle of the store, her breath shallow, her body trembling. The investigator had just given her a warning, and she knew what it meant.

She wasn't safe. She wasn't hidden.

The Runaway Bride

The investigator's shadow loomed over her future, and she knew that it was only a matter of time before the truth caught up to her.

Ten

A Game of Shadows

The door to Foster's Books clicked shut behind the investigator, but Elle couldn't shake the feeling that his presence had never really left. The words he had spoken still echoed in her ears, relentless and suffocating. He had seen through her, connected the dots, and now, he was closing in.

Elle stood frozen for a moment, her fingers trembling as she gripped the edge of the counter. He knows who I am. The realization hit her like a brick, a sinking weight pressing down on her chest. She couldn't escape him, not this time.

She glanced toward the window again. The SUV was still there, parked just across the street, its dark windows reflecting the dim light from the store's interior. She hadn't imagined it. He was watching her. Watching the bookstore. Watching her life.

Margaret appeared at her side, her face set in a mixture of confusion and concern. "You alright, Elle?"

Elle swallowed, forcing herself to nod. "Yeah, I'm fine." She cleared her throat, trying to regain her composure. "Just… just didn't expect company."

Margaret's gaze flicked to the door, where the investigator had just left. "You know him?" she asked quietly, her voice a little hesitant.

Elle hesitated. Should she tell Margaret the truth? Should she drag the woman into this nightmare? The last thing she wanted was to put anyone else in danger.

"I've seen him around," Elle said, her voice steady, though her hands were still shaking. "He's been following me for a while now."

Margaret's brow furrowed. "Following you?"

Elle nodded, swallowing her fear. "I don't know who hired him, but he's determined to find me. I think he already knows who I really am."

Margaret's expression softened, and she reached out, placing a hand on Elle's shoulder. "I had no idea. You don't have to explain anything to me, Elle. But you need to be careful. People like that—investigators, they don't just give up."

Elle nodded, feeling a wave of relief mixed with guilt. Margaret didn't seem afraid, but Elle could see the unease in her eyes. It wasn't just the investigator she had to worry about now; it was the consequences of her presence in this town. She had lived her life in the shadows for so long, but she had never truly understood the weight of being hunted until now.

"You're right," Elle said quietly. "I don't know how long I can keep this up. But I can't go back. I can't go back to that life."

Margaret squeezed her shoulder gently. "You don't have to. Just be careful. If you need to go, you don't have to explain anything to me."

Elle forced a small smile. "Thanks. I'll be careful."

Margaret walked away, leaving Elle alone with her thoughts. The store was quiet now, the soft murmur of customers outside the shop the only sound. But the quiet was deceptive, like the calm before a storm.

Elle turned back toward the counter, her eyes catching the reflection in the window. The black SUV was still there, its engine idling in the dim light. She could almost feel the eyes behind the tinted windows, locked on her every move.

They're waiting for me.

She had to leave. Now.

The door opened again, and Elle's heart leaped into her throat. But it wasn't the investigator this time. It was Noah.

He stepped in casually, his hands stuffed into his jacket pockets. He seemed completely unaware of the tension in the air.

"Hey, Elle," he said with a grin, as if everything was perfectly normal. "I thought I'd stop by and say hi. The coffee's on me today."

Elle forced a smile, trying to push the knot of panic in her stomach away. She wasn't ready to deal with Noah—not now, not when everything was falling apart.

"Noah," she said, her voice coming out a little tighter than she intended. "I—I'm not in the mood for coffee today."

He raised an eyebrow, sensing something was off. "You sure? You've been acting strange lately. You look a little... off. Everything okay?"

Elle shifted uncomfortably, her eyes flicking toward the window again. The SUV was still there. Watching. Noah's presence, however innocent it seemed, was starting to feel like another threat.

"I just have a lot on my mind," Elle said, her words carefully measured. "I'm fine."

Noah stepped closer, his gaze still studying her, but this time with more concern than usual. "You don't have to pretend. If you need to talk, I'm here."

Elle shook her head, willing her voice to remain steady. "I

appreciate it, really, but I just need some time alone."

There was a brief silence as Noah stared at her, something flickering in his eyes. He didn't press further, though, just nodded slowly. "Alright. But if you change your mind, you know where to find me."

Elle didn't respond, her attention still caught on the black SUV outside. Noah hesitated for a moment longer, then turned and walked out of the shop, leaving her alone again.

As soon as the door closed behind him, Elle's eyes darted back to the window. The SUV was still there, the driver's seat empty now, but the car had not moved.

She couldn't keep pretending. She couldn't hide anymore. The investigator would not let her go.

Elle's heart raced, and the weight of her next decision felt unbearable. She had to leave this town. The moment she stepped outside, she would be risking it all, but if she stayed—if she remained anywhere near the bookstore—they would find her.

She couldn't afford to wait any longer.

With a deep breath, Elle grabbed her jacket, stuffing her things into the bag she had kept hidden behind the counter. The back exit of the store was the best way out. She knew the alley behind the building well, and the last thing she needed was to be spotted by anyone who might recognize her.

Her footsteps were quick, but quiet as she moved through the back room and out the door. She didn't stop to look around. She didn't dare.

The cold air hit her as she stepped into the alley, her breath visible in the air. She forced herself to move quickly, walking briskly but not running, not drawing attention to herself.

Every instinct screamed at her to hurry, but she kept her pace steady, controlled. She couldn't afford to look suspicious.

Elle's mind raced as she navigated the backstreets of the town, her eyes darting over her shoulder every few steps. The SUV was still there—it was following her now. She could feel it, the tension, the predatory nature of the chase. The investigator wasn't giving up. He was closing in.

She turned a corner, then another, and then another, trying to lose the vehicle, trying to throw off whoever was watching her. But no matter how many twists and turns she made, no matter how fast she walked, she could still sense that SUV behind her—always lurking just out of sight.

Her chest tightened. He was relentless.

Elle made her way toward the edge of town, hoping for a break, hoping that she might find a way to lose the investigator. But as she passed a row of abandoned buildings, the sound of tires screeching on asphalt broke through the silence. She turned just in time to see the SUV slam around the corner, its headlights cutting through the dark.

It was him.

He had found her again.

Eleven

The Confrontation

The sound of the SUV's tires screeching on the damp pavement was the only thing Elle could hear now. The adrenaline surged through her veins, sending her heart hammering in her chest. She hadn't been able to lose him. She had tried, twisted through alleyways and empty streets, ducking behind corners and through shadowed paths, but the investigator had been relentless—always one step behind.

She knew he would find her eventually. It was only a matter of time. But standing there, in the cold night air, she realized she hadn't truly prepared for this moment. She hadn't prepared for him.

The SUV's headlights glared toward her like twin beams of accusation. Her pulse shot up, the pit of her stomach heavy with the certainty that this was it.

The Confrontation

Elle's thoughts raced, but her feet didn't move. The last thing she wanted was to appear panicked. She needed to stay calm, stay composed. But that was proving to be nearly impossible.

The car stopped a few feet from her, the engine humming quietly as the headlights washed over her. She could feel the presence of the investigator even before the door opened. She hadn't been able to escape him. And now—he was here.

The door clicked open, and the tall figure of the investigator emerged, stepping into the dark street with a slow, deliberate gait. The black coat he wore hung loosely, the collar turned up, his face shadowed beneath the brim of a baseball cap.

For a moment, he said nothing. He simply watched her.

Elle stood frozen, her breath catching in her throat. She couldn't hide from him anymore, couldn't outrun him. He had found her.

"Vivienne," the investigator's voice was calm, but it held an edge of something darker. "I've been looking for you."

Elle's hands clenched into fists at her sides. His words were not a question—they were an accusation. Her old name—Vivienne Sinclair—stung her like a brand. It was the name of a woman she used to be, a woman she had tried so hard to leave behind.

"I'm not Vivienne," Elle said, her voice firm, but even to her own ears, it sounded thin, like a lie barely held together. She forced herself to meet his eyes. "I'm Elle Monroe."

The investigator didn't flinch. "That's a good story, Vivienne. But it doesn't change who you really are."

Her breath hitched. "You don't know who I am," she said, her voice rising a little.

His eyes narrowed. "Oh, I know. And I'm going to make sure everyone else knows too, if it comes to that. But I'd rather not take that route. I'd rather you come with me willingly."

Elle's heart pounded. Willingly? There was nothing about this situation that made her want to go anywhere with him. She wasn't going back.

The silence stretched between them, the tension so thick she could almost taste it. His words hung in the air, a warning wrapped in veiled politeness. He was trying to manipulate her, trying to make her feel like there was a choice. But there was no choice. Not really.

"I'm not going anywhere with you," Elle said, her voice trembling with defiance.

He took a step closer, the cold night air rushing between them. She could feel the space closing in, like he was boxing her in. The weight of his presence was crushing.

"You don't get to decide that, Vivienne," the investigator said softly, almost gently. But there was no kindness in his eyes. Only a cold determination. "You belong to a life you can't outrun. And I'm here to make sure you face the consequences

The Confrontation

of running away."

Elle's mind spun. Consequences. She had made her escape—her great escape—but it seemed like the past was catching up with her, faster than she could run. She thought she was free. She thought she had left everything behind, but now… she was trapped.

The words she had been dreading for months finally spilled from his lips: "Ethan wants you back. He's looking for you, Vivienne. And when he finds you, nothing will stop him from making you pay for what you did."

A cold wave of fear washed over her. Ethan—Ethan Harrington—hadn't just let her go. Of course he hadn't. He had too much at stake. He wanted her back, and the thought of that made Elle's insides twist in a way she couldn't ignore. The thought of returning to him, to the life she had run from, made her want to scream.

"I'm not going back to him," Elle said, her voice firmer now. She straightened, trying to hold her ground, but her heart was a chaotic mess in her chest. She couldn't go back to that life. She wouldn't.

The investigator studied her for a moment, his expression unreadable. "You think you have a choice in this? You're running, Vivienne. You're running from everything. But that's not how this works. The Sinclair name, your family, Ethan—they won't let you go. Not forever."

The Runaway Bride

"I don't care about that," Elle said, her voice fierce, desperate. "I don't care about my family or Ethan. I'm not going back to that. I'm not going back to being someone I'm not. I'm free. I am Elle Monroe now, and I'm not going to let you take that away from me."

For a split second, she thought she saw a flicker of something in the investigator's eyes—a hint of understanding, maybe even a spark of regret. But it vanished quickly, replaced by the cold, emotionless gaze of someone who had a job to do.

"I'm not here to argue with you, Vivienne. I'm here to do my job. And if you don't come with me willingly, I'll have to make you."

Elle's blood ran cold. The threat in his voice was unmistakable. She didn't know what kind of power he had—how far he could push—but she knew one thing for certain: he wouldn't stop until he had her.

Her eyes flicked toward the alley, her mind racing. She could run. She had always been able to run. But was it worth the risk? Was it even possible to outrun him anymore?

But as she considered her options, something shifted in her. A surge of defiance rose up inside her, stronger than the fear. She wasn't going to be controlled by fear any longer. She wasn't going to let this man dictate her future. She was done running.

"I'm not going with you," Elle said, her voice quiet but resolute. "If you think you can force me, then you don't know who you're

The Confrontation

dealing with."

The investigator's expression hardened. "You've made a mistake, Vivienne."

Without warning, he lunged toward her, reaching for her arm. Elle's instincts kicked in. She sidestepped, barely avoiding his grasp. She darted to the side, her heart pounding in her ears.

The investigator swore under his breath, stepping back, but the anger in his eyes was unmistakable. "You think you can outrun me?" he spat, his voice low and threatening. "I'll find you, no matter where you hide. You don't get to escape your past."

Elle didn't answer. She turned and broke into a run. She had to get away. She couldn't stay here, not with him, not with the weight of her past closing in on her.

She could hear his footsteps behind her as she raced down the street, her legs pumping furiously, the cold air burning in her lungs. She wasn't fast enough, though. His shadow loomed over her, and soon she felt the pressure of his pursuit closing in.

A hand gripped her shoulder from behind, and Elle screamed in panic, twisting in his grip, trying to break free. But he was too strong. He shoved her against the nearest wall, pinning her there.

"Let go of me!" Elle shouted, struggling. But his grip tightened, his body pressing her harder into the cold stone.

The Runaway Bride

"You can run all you want, Vivienne," the investigator said, his voice low and menacing. "But you'll never outrun your past. Never."

She was trapped, cornered. There was nowhere left to hide. He had her.

Twelve

The Escape

T he cold stone wall pressed against Elle's back as the investigator's hand tightened around her shoulder. His grip was strong, unyielding, and for a moment, she felt the world tilt beneath her feet. The familiar surge of panic crawled up her throat, but she refused to give in to it. She had fought too long, too hard, to lose everything now.

"Let go of me," she said, her voice trembling but filled with defiance. She tried to twist out of his grasp, but his other hand was already gripping her wrist, pulling her tighter into him. His body was too close, his breath too hot against her ear. She could feel the weight of his presence, like a predator closing in on its prey.

"You're not going anywhere," he said, his voice low and firm, almost as if he were making a promise. His eyes searched hers, cold and calculating. "I've been hired to bring you back, Vivienne. You can't outrun me."

Elle's mind raced, but the thought that kept repeating itself was a simple one: You have to get away.

She couldn't let him take her back to that life. She couldn't go back to Ethan, to the suffocating world that had been mapped out for her before she ever had a say in it. The life of a perfect billionaire's wife. The life of a woman who had no voice. She had fled, and she wasn't going back.

Her eyes darted around frantically, searching for anything, any way to break free. She could feel the cold metal of the alley's trash can against her leg, and an idea struck her. It was dangerous, but it was the only chance she had.

With every ounce of strength she had, Elle kicked the trash can toward the investigator. He was too focused on her to notice, and the force of the metal can crashing into his shin was enough to make him loosen his grip on her arm for just a split second. That was all she needed.

Elle yanked her arm free, using the momentum to shove him back. He stumbled, caught off guard by her unexpected move, and she didn't waste a second. She bolted.

Her heart pounded in her chest, the sound of her feet slapping against the pavement like a drumbeat in her ears. She didn't look back. She couldn't. She just needed to run—run far enough, fast enough that she could lose him.

The Escape

The alley stretched in front of her, dark and narrow, the end just out of sight. The streetlights flickered, casting long shadows over the path. She wasn't familiar with the alleyways here, but she knew the layout of Willow Springs well enough to find her way to the outskirts, where the shadows could cover her long enough for her to disappear.

But the investigator wasn't far behind. She could hear his footsteps pounding on the pavement behind her, growing louder, closer. He wasn't giving up, not now. He had caught her once, and now, he was determined to make sure she didn't slip away again.

She darted down another alley, her breath coming in quick gasps as she took sharp turns, trying to confuse him, trying to lose him in the maze of backstreets. But she could feel him, always just behind her, the echo of his footsteps relentless. He was closing in. She needed a way out.

Ahead of her, the alley opened up to a wider street, and the dim glow of streetlights spilled across the pavement. She knew that if she reached the open road, it would be impossible to disappear. She needed to stay in the shadows.

A door on the left caught her eye. It was old, rusted, and barely hanging on its hinges, but it was a doorway, a possible escape. Without thinking, Elle sprinted toward it. Her hand grasped the handle, twisting with desperation. It creaked loudly in protest, but it opened. She dashed inside, slamming the door behind her.

She leaned against it, chest heaving, her breathing ragged. She had made it inside. For now, she was hidden. But the question was—where was she?

Elle took a cautious step forward, her eyes adjusting to the darkness inside. She could barely make out the outlines of old furniture and broken shelves. It smelled of dust and stale air, the remnants of a place long forgotten.

She crept deeper into the room, trying to calm her racing heart. The silence was oppressive, thick with the weight of uncertainty.

Then, she heard it—the sound of footsteps outside the door. The investigator was still out there. He had found her. He hadn't stopped chasing her, even for a moment.

Her eyes darted around the room, searching for something to use. A window, a hidden exit—anything.

But there was nothing.

The footsteps were getting closer. She could hear the investigator muttering to himself outside, no doubt trying to figure out where she had gone. He wouldn't stop until he found her.

Her eyes settled on a small window above the sink. It was dusty, the glass grimy, but it was a way out. She rushed toward it, her fingers fumbling for the latch. It was stuck, jammed shut from years of disuse. Panic surged again as she yanked on it, but it wouldn't budge.

The Escape

Then—a sound. The door. He was trying it now.

Elle's heart slammed in her chest. She had seconds—maybe less. She couldn't think. She couldn't afford to.

With one final, desperate tug, the window opened with a loud creak. She gasped, her pulse in her throat, and without another thought, she threw herself through the opening.

The cold night air hit her like a slap as she tumbled into the alley behind the building. She landed hard on the ground, her knees scraping against the rough asphalt. Pain shot through her body, but she didn't stop. She couldn't stop.

Elle pushed herself to her feet, her legs shaking, and started running again. The alley was narrow, winding, a network of dead ends and hidden spaces. She could hear the investigator's footsteps pounding after her. He was close. Too close. But she had a head start now, and she wasn't about to let it go to waste.

The sounds of the town grew distant as she took another corner, barely glancing over her shoulder. She couldn't look back. She couldn't risk it. The more time she spent looking behind her, the more he would close in.

But then—there it was. The road ahead. The street that led toward the forest. If she could make it there, she might lose him. The trees, the darkness—they would hide her.

Elle sprinted toward it, pushing her body harder than she ever had before. Her lungs burned, and her muscles screamed in protest, but she didn't slow down. She couldn't.

The road was just ahead now, and as she reached it, the trees loomed in front of her like a dark refuge. She darted into the woods, the cover of the branches above her blocking out the streetlights.

The sound of her footsteps, muffled by the earth beneath her, was the only noise in the oppressive silence. She couldn't see anything in the darkness, but she could feel the trees around her, the rough bark against her fingers as she pushed through the underbrush.

But just as she thought she was safe, she heard it. A voice.

"Vivienne!"

The investigator's shout echoed through the trees. His voice was distant now, but it was getting closer. He was following her. He was closing in.

Elle's heart dropped, and for a moment, she thought she might collapse right there in the woods. But she couldn't afford to stop. Not now. Not when she was so close.

She was free. She was still free.

And she was going to stay that way.

Thirteen

The Truth

The forest around Elle was a blur, her breath coming in sharp gasps as she pushed herself harder, faster, through the undergrowth. The investigator's voice still echoed in her mind, his shout lingering in the cold air, calling her by the name she had abandoned. Vivienne Sinclair. The name was like a brand, searing through her thoughts, dragging her back to a past she had tried to leave behind.

She couldn't stop.

The trees blurred around her as she ran, the rough branches scraping against her arms and legs. Her heart thundered in her chest, but she didn't slow down. She couldn't. Not until she was deep enough in the forest to be lost to him completely.

Behind her, the sounds of pursuit grew fainter, but the thought of stopping—of letting her guard down for even a second—terrified her. She didn't know how long she'd been running, but her legs burned with the effort. She couldn't remember the last time she'd pushed herself this far, this hard. Every step was a battle, but she couldn't stop. She had to keep moving.

And then, she stumbled.

Her foot caught on a root, and she pitched forward, her hands bracing against the ground just in time to keep herself from falling. Her heart pounded in her ears as she pushed herself back to her feet, her breath ragged. She glanced behind her, but the woods were still silent. No footsteps, no voices.

For a moment, Elle stood there, gasping for air, her body shaking. She wiped the sweat from her brow, her eyes scanning the shadows. The sounds of the night—the rustling of leaves, the calls of distant animals—were the only things she could hear.

But even in the quiet of the woods, something didn't feel right.

Elle's instincts told her to keep moving, to keep running until she was far from the investigator and the life she had tried so hard to escape. But something tugged at her, a nagging feeling in the pit of her stomach that wouldn't let go.

Her thoughts turned to Noah, the quiet, easy-going man who had come into her life with the promise of normalcy, of something safe. He had offered her a small escape, a moment of peace amidst the chaos of her world. She had told herself

The Truth

that it was enough—just a moment, a break from the life she had once lived. But now, with the investigator hot on her trail, with everything she had worked for hanging by a thread, she wondered if that was ever enough.

She needed to know. She needed to understand if she was running from something even worse than the investigator.

Noah.

The realization hit her like a thunderclap. She had never told him the truth. Not the whole truth. She had told him bits and pieces, painted a picture of a simple girl running away from a life she no longer wanted, but she had never fully opened up. Never let him in. She had kept the truth buried, hidden under layers of lies.

And now, it was too late. The investigator knew. Ethan knew. And no one would let her hide forever.

But could Noah—could he have been a part of this, too?

A cold shiver ran down her spine as the thought settled in. What if Noah had known all along? What if he was simply another pawn in the game Ethan had set in motion? She couldn't shake the nagging doubt that maybe, just maybe, Noah had been watching her, all along.

Elle pushed the thought aside, not wanting to believe it. Noah had seemed different. He had been kind to her, had treated her like a normal person—not like a prisoner. But what if he had been playing a part in something she didn't understand? Something much bigger than her. Something she had underestimated.

Her mind spiraled as she pushed forward, the thick underbrush slowing her down. She was desperate for answers, but all she could think of now was the way the investigator's eyes had looked at her when he'd cornered her in the alley. The way he'd said, "You can't outrun your past."

Maybe he was right. Maybe she couldn't outrun it.

Elle's breath hitched as she felt something cold settle deep within her chest. She had thought she could run, that she could leave it all behind. But the more she tried to escape, the more she realized that her past was chasing her. It had always been chasing her.

And then, as if on cue, the sound of footsteps reached her ears. They were faint at first, but unmistakable. The crunch of leaves underfoot. The snap of twigs.

Elle froze, her heart skipping a beat.

She whipped her head around, scanning the darkness, her breath catching in her throat. Her first instinct was to run, but she forced herself to stay still, her back pressed against the rough bark of a nearby tree. She barely dared to breathe, straining her ears for the slightest sound.

The footsteps were getting closer.

The Truth

Elle's mind raced. Who was it? Was it the investigator? Had he tracked her down already? Or was it someone else?

Her hands trembled as she pressed them to her sides. The forest around her seemed to close in, the shadows darkening, the air thick with tension. She could feel her pulse racing in her throat, could hear the blood pounding in her ears.

The footsteps were only a few feet away now.

Then—a voice.

"Elle."

Her breath caught in her chest. It was a voice she recognized—Noah.

She didn't move. She didn't dare.

"Elle," Noah called again, his voice low, but tinged with something she couldn't quite place. "I know you're out there."

Elle's chest tightened, and for a moment, she stood there, frozen in place, unsure of what to do. Should she run? Should she hide? Should she confront him?

Noah's voice cut through the silence again, this time a little closer. "I'm not going to hurt you."

She didn't believe him. She couldn't. Not now.

Elle swallowed the knot in her throat and stepped out from behind the tree, her body tense, her breath shallow. She couldn't hide anymore. She couldn't keep running.

She emerged into the clearing, the moonlight casting long shadows over the forest floor. Noah stood there, his hands in his pockets, his expression unreadable. He wasn't close—still a good ten feet away from her. But his presence felt like it was closing in on her, like his eyes were tearing through the carefully constructed walls she had built around herself.

"Why are you following me?" Elle demanded, her voice trembling with a mixture of fear and anger. "What do you want from me?"

Noah didn't answer right away. Instead, he took a step toward her, his eyes softening for just a moment. "Elle, you don't understand. I never meant for any of this to happen."

Elle's heart thudded painfully in her chest. "What does that mean? What's going on? Why did you pretend to be—" She paused, the words catching in her throat. "Why didn't you tell me the truth?"

Noah's eyes flickered with something like regret, but his expression was still guarded. "It's not what you think. I—" He broke off, his gaze darting around the clearing, as if he was afraid someone else might be listening.

Elle stepped back, shaking her head. "You're lying. You've been lying this whole time."

The Truth

"No, Elle," Noah said, his voice urgent. "It's complicated. I never wanted to hurt you. But Ethan—he's been looking for you. I was hired to keep an eye on you."

Elle's stomach dropped. "What?"

The truth crashed over her in an avalanche, and she felt the world go numb. She had trusted him. She had let him in, let him believe she was something she wasn't. She had let him offer her an escape. And now—now he had been part of the lie all along.

"I didn't want to, but I was—" Noah started, but Elle held up a hand, cutting him off.

"Stop," she said, her voice raw, the tears threatening to spill. "I can't... I can't do this anymore."

She turned to run, to leave him behind, but this time, she didn't know if she could outrun the truth.

Fourteen

The Betrayal

Elle's breath came in shallow, uneven gasps as she turned and sprinted into the woods, the sound of Noah's voice echoing behind her, growing fainter with every step she took. The betrayal was sharp, cutting through her like a knife. She had trusted him. She had believed in the simplicity of their moments together—the quiet coffee breaks, the shared smiles, the fleeting moments where she felt like maybe, just maybe, she could be something other than a fugitive. But now, standing at the edge of the forest, she realized how foolish that belief had been. He was no different than the others—just another part of the trap.

She couldn't trust anyone.

She pushed through the dense underbrush, the thick trees growing closer together, their branches reaching down like

The Betrayal

skeletal hands trying to hold her back. But she didn't stop. She couldn't. If she did, she would break, and the truth would crush her. The truth that Noah had known all along, that he had played his part in the elaborate lie, the game of deceit she had been trapped in since the moment she ran away.

The deeper into the woods she ran, the harder it became to breathe. The damp air of the forest clung to her skin, and her thoughts were a chaotic mess—images of Noah's face, the look in his eyes when he admitted the truth. Ethan had sent him. Ethan. The man she had once loved, the man who had controlled her every move, who had set the stage for everything she had done, everything she had been. And now, here she was, running again—running from him, from everything.

No, she couldn't go back to him.

She wouldn't go back to that life, not to the cold, suffocating mansion, not to the promises of a life she never asked for. She was Elle Monroe now—not Vivienne Sinclair. She would not be a puppet, manipulated by those who saw her as nothing more than a prize to be won.

But where could she go?

The question nagged at her, a constant shadow in her mind. The woods, dark and endless, seemed like a good place to hide, but for how long? She had no plan, no strategy. No way out.

Elle slowed, her lungs burning as she stumbled to a halt. Her knees buckled, and she sank to the damp ground, gasping for air. She had to think. She had to come up with something. She couldn't let Noah find her again. She couldn't let him—anyone—find her.

The weight of her own thoughts, her overwhelming emotions, nearly crushed her. She had been a fool. She had let her guard down, believed that she could find solace, even for a moment. But that was before she learned the truth—before she realized that everything had been a lie. Noah's kindness, his smile, had all been part of the same game.

She squeezed her eyes shut, trying to shut out the memories of the last few days—the way he had looked at her, the way she had confided in him, the way she had believed they had a chance at something real. But it had all been a lie.

A rustling sound to her left snapped Elle's eyes open. Her body stiffened, adrenaline shooting through her veins as she scrambled to her feet. Her mind raced, every instinct screaming for her to flee. It was him.

Her heart pounded as she turned to face the direction of the sound, her hands trembling. She couldn't see anything—just the dark shadows of trees, the thick underbrush blocking her view.

A figure stepped forward into the clearing. Elle's breath caught in her throat as she took a step back, her pulse spiking. It wasn't the investigator this time.

It was Noah.

The Betrayal

His figure was barely visible in the darkness, but she could make out his silhouette as he stood motionless, watching her. His eyes were trained on her, and despite the distance between them, Elle felt the weight of his gaze, heavy and suffocating.

"Elle," he called softly, his voice hoarse, as if he hadn't spoken in days. His tone was genuine, but it made her sick to hear it. "Please, just stop running. You don't have to do this."

Elle clenched her fists, a surge of anger rising in her chest. How dare he? After everything he had just revealed to her, after everything he had lied about, how dare he speak to her like that?

"I don't want to talk to you," Elle said, her voice shaking with fury. She turned to leave, her feet stumbling in the dark, but Noah's next words made her stop dead in her tracks.

"You don't understand. It wasn't supposed to happen like this." His voice cracked slightly, and for a moment, Elle almost believed him. "I never wanted you to get caught up in all of this. I never wanted to hurt you."

Elle's head whipped around to face him, her expression hard. "You don't get to apologize now. You don't get to act like I'm some helpless victim in your little game, Noah. You've been a part of it all along, haven't you? You were watching me, waiting for the moment when I'd slip up, when I'd reveal myself."

Noah took a step forward, his face now illuminated by the faint moonlight. His eyes were full of regret, but Elle didn't care. She didn't care about his remorse. She didn't care that he seemed to want to make things right. He had betrayed her.

"I wasn't watching you," he said, his voice shaking now. "I was trying to keep you safe. I—I thought if I could get close enough, if I could keep you from running, maybe I could protect you from them. From Ethan."

Elle's breath hitched, a bitter laugh escaping her lips. "Protect me? From Ethan? By lying to me? By hiding the truth?" She stepped forward, her voice rising with every word. "You were just another part of his plan. I was never anything more than a pawn to you both."

Noah flinched as though her words physically struck him. His eyes darkened, and for a moment, Elle saw the raw vulnerability in his expression. "I never wanted to be part of his plan," he said quietly, his voice barely above a whisper. "But I was. I couldn't stop it."

Elle shook her head, the pain of betrayal cutting through her, sharp and deep. She couldn't breathe through it. She couldn't understand how she had been so blind, how she had trusted him so completely.

"You don't get it," Elle said, her voice cracking. "I'm done with that life. I'm done running, done hiding, done being someone else's possession. You… you were supposed to be my escape. And now you're just another reminder of how trapped I am."

Noah reached out, his hand trembling as if he wanted to touch her, to make her listen. "Elle, please. Just hear me out—"

"No!" Elle snapped, stepping back, away from him. "You don't get to explain this away. You've already betrayed me." Her voice was trembling with raw emotion now, every word heavy with the weight of everything she had discovered. "There is no excuse for that."

The silence between them stretched, heavy and thick with the unspoken truth that lay in the air, unacknowledged but undeniable. She could see it in his eyes—the pain, the regret, but also the resignation. He knew. He knew she would never forgive him. Not after everything.

"I tried to stop them," Noah said quietly, his voice thick with emotion. "I tried to warn you. But there's only so much I could do. They were coming for you, Elle, whether you wanted it or not."

Elle turned away, unable to look at him anymore. "I don't care. I don't care about your excuses." She swallowed hard, her throat tight. "I don't want your protection. I don't need it. I just need you to leave me alone."

There was a long pause, and then Noah sighed heavily. "I can't do that. I can't just walk away and leave you to face this alone." His voice was soft, filled with emotion she couldn't decipher. "Please. Let me help you."

Elle turned to face him one last time, her eyes cold and distant. "There's nothing left for you to help me with, Noah. I've already made my decision. I don't need your help. I don't need anyone's help."

For the briefest of moments, Noah seemed to search her face, his expression torn. But then, as if some invisible wall came crashing down between them, he nodded. "I can't stop you from running. But you're not alone in this, Elle."

With that, he turned and disappeared into the shadows of the forest, leaving her standing alone in the dark, her heart in pieces.

As the silence settled once more, Elle felt the weight of the betrayal in her chest, heavy and suffocating. She was alone.

And this time, it wasn't just in the woods.

This time, she was completely, utterly, alone.

Fifteen

Into the Abyss

The forest seemed to stretch endlessly in front of Elle, the shadows of the trees dancing as a light breeze rustled the leaves above. The night felt impossibly still, as if the very earth beneath her feet was holding its breath, waiting for something to happen.

Elle had been running for what felt like hours, but now, as she stood alone in the clearing, everything had ground to a halt. The weight of Noah's words still lingered in the air, thick and suffocating. He had tried to protect her, he said. He had tried to stop them, but now, he was gone, disappeared into the same night that seemed to close in on her. And in that moment, she realized the terrible truth: there was no one left to protect her.

Her chest tightened, a sharp pang of loneliness and betrayal gnawing at her heart. She had trusted him. She had let him in, had allowed herself to believe that there was someone in her corner, someone who understood her, someone who wouldn't betray her. But now she knew better. She was just another piece in a game far bigger than her.

Elle closed her eyes, forcing herself to focus, to breathe. There was no time for regret, no time for weakness. She had run once before. She had broken free of Ethan, of the life she had been trapped in. But now? Now, it felt like the walls were closing in again, tighter and tighter, and she wasn't sure if she had the strength to fight anymore.

The chill of the night air wrapped around her like a cloak, and she drew her jacket tighter against her body. The silence of the forest was deafening, but it wasn't the silence she feared. It was the waiting. The knowing that someone was out there, hunting her.

The investigator.

Ethan.

Noah.

They were all coming for her.

She needed a plan.

Elle turned, looking around at the dark woods stretching out around her. She had to keep moving. She had no other choice. There was no hiding from them—not in the woods, not in the shadows. She was exposed, vulnerable, and if she stayed here much longer, they would find her.

But she wasn't ready to give up. Not yet. Not when she could still feel the faint, lingering hope in her chest that there had to be a way out, a way to make them stop chasing her.

Her mind raced as she moved deeper into the forest, the crunch of her boots against the fallen leaves the only sound in the otherwise quiet night. She was too exposed here, too easy to spot. She needed cover, something to shield her from view, something that would give her a chance to think and plan her next move.

As she trudged forward, a shadow darted in the corner of her eye, and her body immediately went on alert. She froze, heart pounding in her chest, her breath caught in her throat. Her eyes searched the darkness, trying to find the source of the movement, but there was nothing.

A branch cracked behind her.

Elle spun around, panic surging through her veins. She had been too careless. She had been too focused on her thoughts, and now, someone was right behind her.

Before she could react, a figure emerged from the darkness, stepping forward into the moonlight. Elle's heart stopped.

It was Noah.

But he wasn't alone. Behind him stood a tall, broad-shouldered man. His face was shadowed by the brim of a hat, but there was no mistaking the presence of the investigator.

Noah's gaze locked with hers, and for a split second, his eyes softened. "Elle," he said, his voice almost a whisper, full of regret and apology. "You don't have to run anymore."

Elle's breath caught in her throat. She took a step back, her legs weak, her pulse quickening in fear. "Noah—" She couldn't bring herself to say his name, not when she saw the other man standing there, not when she realized just how deep this betrayal ran.

The investigator took a step forward, his gaze locking onto hers with cold, calculating eyes. "You've been running for too long, Vivienne," he said, his voice smooth, almost polite. "It's time to stop."

Elle's chest tightened. There was no place left to run. No corner to hide in. She had no idea how they had found her, how they had caught up to her so quickly, but she knew—this was it.

She felt the weight of the situation, the inevitability of it all crashing down on her. She was trapped. And it was because of Noah.

"Why?" Elle asked, her voice barely above a whisper. "Why didn't you just leave me alone?" Her eyes flickered to the investigator, then back to Noah. "You were supposed to protect me." The words came out bitter, full of the anger that had been building inside her ever since she learned the truth.

Noah looked at her, his jaw clenched, but he didn't speak. He didn't try to defend himself. He knew she wouldn't forgive him.

The investigator stepped forward again, this time with an unsettling calmness. "She's not going anywhere, Noah," he said, his voice cold. "We're bringing her back."

Elle took a step back, her hands raised instinctively. "No," she whispered. "You can't. I won't go back. I won't." Her voice grew louder, more desperate. "I don't belong to any of you. You can't make me go back. Not to him. Not to any of it. I'm not Vivienne Sinclair anymore."

The investigator's eyes glinted with something dangerous as he stepped closer, his hand resting on the grip of the gun holstered at his side. "You don't have a choice," he said, his tone final. "You're coming with us, whether you like it or not."

The reality of his words hit Elle with full force, and she felt her blood run cold. There was no escape this time. No clever tricks, no more running. She was cornered, trapped in a web of lies and deceit, a puppet in someone else's twisted game.

"Noah," Elle said, her voice cracking with emotion. "Help me."

Noah's face softened for a brief moment, but the look in his eyes was conflicted, torn. She could see it now—the guilt, the regret, and maybe even the hint of compassion. But there was also fear. Fear of what Ethan, of what the investigator, would do to him if he didn't cooperate.

"Elle," he whispered, his voice strained. "I can't help you. Not anymore."

The words hit Elle harder than anything else he could have said. She took another step back, feeling the ground beneath her shift. This was it. The walls were closing in.

"You've already betrayed me," Elle said, her voice cold with rage. "I can't trust you anymore."

The investigator's hand twitched at his side, and in an instant, Elle knew what he was about to do. She could see the danger in his eyes, the predatory glint that made her stomach churn.

"No," Elle said, her voice rising in panic. "No, please."

But the investigator was already moving. He stepped forward and grabbed her arm, pulling her toward him with brutal force. Elle fought against his grip, twisting and struggling, but his hold was ironclad. She kicked at his legs, her nails scratching at his hands, but nothing worked. His strength was too much.

"No!" she screamed again, her voice raw with desperation.

Noah moved to step forward, his hand outstretched as though he wanted to stop the investigator, but then he froze. Elle's eyes locked with his, and for a second, she saw something in his gaze—a flicker of the man she thought she had known. But that was all it was—a fleeting illusion.

"Let go of me!" Elle shouted, her voice breaking as the investigator dragged her toward the trees, his grip unyielding.

The sound of her own pulse thrumming in her ears was the only thing she could hear now. The world around her felt distant, unreal. She had failed. She had fought as hard as she could, but it wasn't enough. They were taking her back.

Back to the life she had run from.

As the investigator pulled her away, she glanced at Noah one last time. His face was etched with regret, but his eyes—his eyes held nothing for her now. Not the hope, not the kindness. Nothing.

Elle closed her eyes, a wave of despair crashing over her.

It was over.

And the truth had never been so heavy.

Sixteen

Escape Plan

Elle's heart was pounding in her chest, each beat echoing louder than the footsteps of the man dragging her through the thick underbrush of the forest. She stumbled, her foot catching on the rough ground, but the investigator's grip on her arm tightened, dragging her forward. The night felt endless—cold and suffocating, and the weight of the world seemed to press down on her chest with every step. She had failed. She had let herself get cornered, and now they were taking her back. There was no escaping this time.

"No!" Elle gasped, her voice trembling with desperation as she dug her heels into the earth. "Let me go! I won't go back!"

The investigator's eyes glinted with a cold resolve. "You don't have a choice, Vivienne," he said, his voice smooth and unwavering. "Ethan is waiting. You're going back whether you want to or not."

Elle's mind raced, her thoughts spinning as she tried to push against his grip. She had always believed that if she ran far enough, she could outrun her past. But now, as he pulled her deeper into the woods, the truth settled heavily around her: Ethan had found her, and there was no escape.

The trees seemed to close in on her, their dark branches reaching out like long fingers, a forest of shadows swallowing her whole. The investigator's footsteps were the only sound that broke the silence, steady and determined as he led her toward something she couldn't see, but knew was waiting.

Suddenly, she felt the ground shift beneath her. Her feet slid in the dirt, and for a brief moment, her body went slack in his grip.

"Please," Elle begged, the words slipping out before she could stop herself. "Please, I can't go back to him. I can't... I can't be Vivienne anymore. I'm not her. I'm not."

The investigator stopped, his grip loosening slightly, but only for a second. He turned to face her, his cold eyes staring down at her with an almost pitying look. "I don't care who you think you are, Vivienne," he said, his voice hard. "I don't care what name you've given yourself. You belong to him. And you'll answer to him."

Elle's pulse surged in her ears as she struggled against his hold. She couldn't let him take her back. She couldn't let them win.

The Runaway Bride

The memories of the life she had fled—the cold dinners, the suffocating events, the promises made on her behalf—flashed before her eyes. But something else was flashing too, a moment of clarity in the chaos. She could still fight. She had to fight.

Without warning, Elle spun around, using the force of the sudden movement to break free of his grip. She kicked backward, her boot connecting with his shin. He stumbled, and in that brief instant of chaos, Elle didn't waste a second. She turned and sprinted through the trees, ignoring the sharp branches that scratched at her skin, the rocks that tripped her feet. She wasn't going to stop this time. She couldn't stop.

She ran faster than she ever had before, the cold night air filling her lungs, her mind consumed with one thought: Get away.

Behind her, she heard the investigator's shouts, but they only pushed her forward, driving her deeper into the forest. She didn't know where she was going. She didn't know if she was heading toward safety or deeper into danger, but it didn't matter. All that mattered was that she was free. For now.

Her feet slapped against the dirt path, the sound of her own breath filling her ears as she pushed through the thick underbrush. The world around her was a blur—just trees, just darkness. The smell of pine and damp earth filled her nostrils, and the sound of her heartbeat thudded in her chest, louder than anything else.

She could hear his footsteps behind her now—louder, faster—he was closing in. But Elle didn't stop. She couldn't stop.

And then, a noise to her left—a crack of a twig, the rustle of leaves—and Elle froze, her heart jumping into her throat. She looked to the side, half-expecting to see the investigator, but what she saw instead made her blood run cold.

Noah.

He was standing there, partially hidden behind the thick trunks of the trees, his eyes locked onto hers. His face was pale, his expression unreadable, but there was something in his eyes—something that made Elle's chest tighten.

"Noah," she breathed, almost as if the word were a plea. "What are you doing here?"

Noah didn't speak at first. He just watched her, his gaze intense, full of guilt and regret. He didn't move forward, didn't reach out. Instead, he looked at her as if trying to gauge her, his lips pressed together in a tight line.

"Elle," he said quietly, his voice barely above a whisper, "You don't understand."

Elle's heart raced, her mind spinning. She felt like she was being pulled in two directions. Part of her wanted to run to him, to beg him for help, to ask for the protection he had promised her so many times before. But another part of her, the part that had been betrayed, knew better.

"Noah, you're part of this. You lied to me," she said, her voice shaking with the weight of everything she had learned. "You've been part of this from the beginning. I—I trusted you." Her words were thick with emotion, raw and painful.

Noah stepped forward slightly, but he didn't reach for her. He didn't touch her. Instead, he stood there, as though weighed down by some heavy truth, some invisible burden. "I never wanted this, Elle. I never wanted you to get caught up in this."

"Then why did you do it?" Elle snapped, her anger boiling over. "Why didn't you just tell me the truth? Why didn't you just leave me alone? You've been playing me this whole time, Noah. You've been watching me, letting them—"

She broke off, unable to finish the sentence. The words felt like they would suffocate her if she said them out loud.

"I didn't have a choice," Noah said quietly, the words coming out in a rush. "I was trying to protect you. I thought if I could keep you close, if I could make sure you didn't run, I could get you out of this. But Ethan's not the kind of man you can just walk away from."

Elle felt a bitter laugh rise in her throat, but she suppressed it. She couldn't let him see her like this—broken, betrayed, vulnerable. Not again.

"I don't need your protection, Noah. I never did," she said, her voice flat, the weight of her anger heavy in the air. "I don't need anyone to protect me. You should have just let me go. You should have just stayed out of it."

The words hung between them like a thick fog. Noah opened his mouth as though to respond, but no sound came out. He just stood there, caught in some invisible conflict, his eyes flicking between her and the investigator, who had finally caught up with them.

"Elle," Noah said softly, almost pleading now, "Please, just listen to me. You're not alone in this. I—I never wanted this to happen, but I couldn't walk away from it. I couldn't let him take you back."

Elle's head spun, the confusion clouding her thoughts. She wanted to believe him. She wanted to believe that there was still something good in him, something worth saving. But she couldn't. Not now. Not after everything he had done.

And then, it all became clear. The investigator, standing in the shadows, his face unreadable, didn't move. He didn't need to. He was waiting. Waiting for Elle to make the wrong choice. Waiting for her to surrender.

And in that moment, Elle knew. She knew that she wasn't going to be able to outrun this anymore. She wasn't going to be able to escape. She had tried—she had fought—but now, there was no choice left.

Her body tensed, and her eyes locked onto Noah one last time.

And then, with a final burst of strength, she turned and ran.

This time, she wasn't running from the investigator, from

Ethan. She wasn't running from Noah.

She was running from the life that had never been hers to begin with.

Seventeen

The Brink of Darkness

Elle's heart hammered in her chest as she sprinted deeper into the woods, her legs burning with the effort. The branches whipped at her face, the rough bark scraping her skin, but she didn't stop. She couldn't stop. Not now.

The sound of her breath was ragged, desperate. Her mind screamed for her to keep moving, to run faster, to leave everything behind. But with every step, every heartbeat, the reality of her situation settled more heavily on her shoulders. She was running out of time, running out of options, and yet, there was no part of her that could stand still, no part of her that could let them take her again.

She glanced over her shoulder, half-expecting to see the investigator close behind her, his face set with cold determination.

But the woods were silent. The night air was heavy, thick with the scent of damp earth and pine, but no sound followed her. She couldn't be sure if they were still chasing her—Noah, the investigator, or Ethan's men. But she couldn't trust the silence. She couldn't trust that she was safe.

The trees blurred as she weaved through them, her footsteps echoing in the dark. The moon barely filtered through the thick canopy above, casting only faint light on the ground. Everything felt like a shadow—a nightmare closing in on her, one step at a time.

No. Not this time. Not again.

Her thoughts raced, every nerve on edge, every muscle screaming for rest, but Elle pushed on. She couldn't afford to stop. She couldn't afford to slow down. The fear, the panic that had gripped her since the moment she realized she was trapped, hadn't loosened its hold. It had only grown tighter. She had been running for so long.

She had once thought that escaping would make everything better, that starting fresh would give her a chance to heal. But now, as she raced through the woods, every shadow seemed to close in tighter, every snap of a twig behind her sending a surge of panic through her chest.

Her breath hitched as her foot caught on a root, and she tumbled forward, hitting the ground hard. The force of the fall knocked the wind out of her, and for a brief moment, she lay there, gasping for air, unable to move.

The Brink of Darkness

Get up, Elle. You can't stop now.

She forced herself to push up, her palms scraping against the dirt as she pushed herself upright. She could feel the sharp sting of the abrasions on her skin, but there was no time to feel sorry for herself. No time to give in to the pain.

The woods around her were suffocating, the silence oppressive. She had no idea how much farther she could go, how much longer she could run. Was she running toward freedom, or deeper into the trap?

Elle stumbled forward again, her legs shaking, but she kept moving. She knew the only way she would get out of this was if she didn't stop. If she could just outrun them for long enough, just long enough to find some kind of escape, some kind of hope.

But the forest was growing darker, the shadows closing in, and she couldn't shake the feeling that something—someone—was watching her.

Suddenly, the sound of footsteps behind her broke the silence. Her heart skipped a beat. She hadn't imagined it. She wasn't alone.

Elle's body tensed, her muscles locking as she pivoted and bolted to the side, veering off the path. The underbrush cracked beneath her feet as she dodged branches and thick vines. She could hear them now—footsteps. Close. Too close.

The Runaway Bride

She darted between the trees, every sense alert, but her breath was coming too quickly, too sharply. She couldn't think, couldn't focus. Her mind was spiraling, and every time she heard a sound, she convinced herself they were behind her. But she couldn't look back. She couldn't afford to.

The footsteps grew louder, and then—a voice.

"Elle!"

It wasn't the investigator. It wasn't the man she had fought off. This voice was familiar. Too familiar.

Elle's heart froze. The voice was like a dagger lodged in her chest, a reminder of everything she had been running from.

"Noah..." The name slipped out before she could stop it, the word trembling on her lips.

She skidded to a halt, her eyes darting through the trees. She couldn't see him yet, but she could feel him. His presence, like a ghost, haunting her every step.

"Noah, stay away," she whispered to herself, her voice hoarse with panic. "Stay away. Don't come any closer."

But the sound of footsteps—his footsteps—grew louder. Elle's pulse thundered in her ears, drowning out everything else.

And then, through the darkness, she saw him.

Noah stepped into the clearing, his face grim, his eyes searching for her. The moonlight revealed the lines of fatigue on his face, the worry in his eyes.

"Elle," he called again, his voice strained, almost desperate. "Please, just stop running."

Elle's body froze, her thoughts a chaotic mess. She didn't know what to say, what to do. She had trusted him once. She had believed in him. But now, after everything, she wasn't sure she could ever believe again.

"Noah," she said, her voice tight with emotion. "Why? Why are you here? You should have left me alone."

"I couldn't leave you alone," Noah replied, his voice filled with regret. "You don't understand. They're not going to stop, Elle. They won't stop until they find you. I couldn't—couldn't just let you go on like this. I couldn't watch you run into danger."

Elle shook her head, stepping back, her mind spinning with disbelief. "You were working for them," she said harshly. "You lied to me. You pretended to be someone you weren't. And now you're telling me this?"

"No," Noah said, taking a step forward. His hands were outstretched, palms open, as if pleading with her. "I never wanted to hurt you. I never wanted to be a part of this, but I was. You were being hunted, and I couldn't just stand by and watch."

Elle's chest tightened, the pain of betrayal rising like a tidal wave inside her. "You couldn't stand by and watch?" she repeated, her voice trembling with fury. "You were a part of it, Noah. You were a part of it all along. You were a part of the lie. All of it."

"No, you don't understand!" Noah's voice cracked, and for the first time, Elle saw the vulnerability in his eyes—the guilt, the remorse. "I tried to stop them. I tried to warn you. I wanted to get you out, but I couldn't do it alone. I—"

"Stop!" Elle shouted, the words like a punch in the gut. "Stop lying to me! You've been part of this from the beginning. You let me believe that you cared about me. But it was all just part of their game, wasn't it? You were never on my side."

Noah took a deep breath, stepping closer, his hand reaching out to her, but Elle jerked back, her body rigid with anger and fear.

"I couldn't save you," Noah said, his voice broken. "I couldn't stop them. I'm sorry."

Elle stood there, staring at him, the world spinning around her. Her chest rose and fell with every ragged breath, the weight of his words crushing her. She couldn't speak. She didn't know what to say. The truth was there, right in front of her, but it felt like a final blow.

There was a long silence between them. Elle's breath was shaky, and her hands were trembling. Her entire body felt like it was being ripped apart, torn between the man she had trusted and the man she now knew had betrayed her.

"You're too late," Elle said finally, her voice barely a whisper. "You've already betrayed me, Noah. I can't trust you anymore."

Noah stood there, frozen, unable to move, unable to speak. He opened his mouth as if to say something more, but Elle shook her head, turning away from him.

"You don't have the right to explain anymore," she said, her voice cold, and without another word, she turned and ran again, the sound of Noah's voice calling out to her fading behind her.

Her body was numb, but her mind was clearer than ever. This time, there was no turning back. She wasn't running from just the investigator, from the men who were hunting her. This time, she was running from Noah, from the trust she had placed in him, from everything she had believed.

She was running from the past.

And this time, she wasn't stopping.

Eighteen

Final Stand

The world felt like it was closing in on Elle. The trees blurred as she ran, her legs screaming in protest, the cold air rushing past her face. She could hear her heart pounding in her chest, the rhythm a constant reminder of how much time was slipping through her fingers. Every footfall felt heavier than the last, every breath harder to catch. She had been running for what felt like an eternity, but the distance between her and those chasing her was closing, and she could feel it.

The investigator. Noah. Ethan. They were all closing in, one by one. She could feel their presence even when they weren't close, their shadows hovering over her like a dark cloud that she could never escape.

Elle's mind was racing, a flurry of thoughts and emotions she couldn't shake. She had been betrayed by Noah. The one person she had let into her life. The one person who had promised to help her, to protect her. But now, she was left alone again, her trust shattered, and the path ahead unclear.

Her footsteps faltered as a sharp pain shot through her side. She hadn't stopped running since she broke free of Noah, but her body was nearing its limits. She needed a plan, but the woods felt endless, and she couldn't see a way out. The trees pressed in from all sides, the path too narrow, too winding to provide a clear escape.

For the first time in days, Elle slowed, her breath ragged, her vision blurred with exhaustion. Her mind was spinning. She couldn't outrun them forever, not like this. She was tired. She was scared. And she had no idea where she was going.

Think.

Her pulse thrummed in her ears as she leaned against a large tree, trying to catch her breath. She had to focus. If she didn't, if she let the fear take over, she would never escape. She had been cornered before, but she had always found a way out. She couldn't give up now.

The sound of footsteps broke her concentration. At first, they were faint, almost indistinguishable from the rustling of the wind through the leaves. But they grew louder, more distinct, and Elle's heart skipped a beat. She couldn't hear their voices yet, but she knew—they were coming for her.

The Runaway Bride

Her hands trembled as she pushed off the tree, her body on alert, every muscle taut. It wasn't just the investigator. She could feel Noah's betrayal like a weight in her chest, a crushing pressure that threatened to break her. She didn't know how to feel about him anymore—he had been a part of it all along. But he wasn't here. Not yet. The investigator was. And he was close.

Elle took a step back, her body tensing as the footsteps grew nearer. She had no time to think, no time to plan. She had to move. Her legs screamed as she ran again, darting into the shadows of the trees, hoping that the thick foliage would hide her.

Her breath came in uneven bursts as she sprinted, the pain in her side flaring with every step. She couldn't keep this up forever. But if she stopped now, they would catch her. She had to keep moving.

But the forest seemed to stretch on forever, the shadows growing darker with every passing second. Elle's mind raced as she tried to think of a way to throw them off. She needed a way to make them believe she was going one way when she was really going another. A path. A place to hide.

And then—there it was.

A clearing.

Elle's breath caught in her throat as she saw it in front of her, the trees breaking open to reveal a small, dark cabin at the edge of the clearing. It was old, abandoned. The kind of place someone might use for shelter. The kind of place she could hide.

Her pulse quickened as she headed toward the cabin, her feet moving faster now, almost as if she could feel the walls closing in around her. She didn't have much time. They were so close.

She reached the door, her hands trembling as she pushed it open. It creaked, the sound too loud in the still night, and Elle winced, but she didn't care. She stepped inside, the smell of mildew and dust greeting her, the air stale from years of disuse.

The interior was small, dimly lit by the faint light filtering in through the cracked windows. A wooden table sat in the middle of the room, covered in dust, and a few scattered chairs. The floor creaked beneath her as she stepped further in, her heart racing in her chest.

Where could she hide?

Her eyes scanned the room, settling on a narrow staircase that led to a loft. Without thinking, Elle moved toward it, climbing up the creaky steps as quietly as she could. She didn't know what she was looking for, but she couldn't risk being seen. She had to stay hidden.

At the top of the stairs, the loft was barely big enough to fit a bed, let alone anyone else. It was dark up here, the air thick with dust, but Elle found a small corner near the back, wedged between the wall and the ceiling. She crouched down, pulling

The Runaway Bride

her knees to her chest as she tried to calm her breathing.

Please. Let them pass.

The silence that followed was deafening. Elle strained her ears, listening for any sound—anything that could give her a clue as to where they were. She heard nothing. Just the sounds of the wind rustling through the trees outside, and her own labored breath.

And then—a sound.

Footsteps. Slow, deliberate, and unmistakable.

They had found the cabin.

Elle's heart stopped. She knew they were here. She had no time left. She held her breath, listening as the footsteps drew nearer, louder, closer. She could hear the investigator's voice now, low and commanding.

"Vivienne," he called softly. "We know you're in there. There's nowhere to run. Come out and make this easy."

Elle's pulse thundered in her ears. This was it.

She had no choice. She had to act.

As quietly as she could, she crawled to the edge of the loft, peeking through the cracks in the floorboards. She could see the faint shadow of the investigator moving outside, his silhouette framed against the door.

The cabin was surrounded.

Elle's chest tightened, but she knew she couldn't stay hidden forever. She had to make a move. She had to get out.

She quickly surveyed the loft, her eyes darting over the wooden beams and the narrow openings in the walls. And then, it clicked.

The window.

A small, dirty window sat on the far side of the loft, barely large enough for her to squeeze through. It wasn't much, but it was the only chance she had. If she could make it out without being seen, she might have a shot at escaping—at getting out of the cabin before they could get to her.

Elle moved swiftly, her hands trembling as she pulled herself up to the window. The glass was cracked, the frame old and rusted, but it still opened. She pushed it, wincing as it creaked loudly in the silence, but she didn't stop.

With a final push, she squeezed through the narrow opening, her body scraping against the rough wood as she pushed herself through the gap. Her feet hit the ground outside, and she staggered slightly, but she didn't stop. She couldn't stop.

Elle darted into the forest, her eyes scanning the darkness ahead. There had to be a way out. The trees loomed around her, but she had to keep moving, keep running.

For a moment, the world seemed to blur around her. The sound of footsteps behind her was still there, but it was farther away.

Keep moving.

She didn't know how far she would get, but for the first time in what felt like forever, Elle felt like she had a chance.

She didn't know what awaited her in the dark forest, what dangers were hidden in the shadows. But she knew one thing: she wasn't going down without a fight.

She would not be a prisoner anymore.

And she would never go back.

Nineteen

Brink of Betrayal

The woods were thick with shadows, and the air was so heavy with tension that Elle could almost taste it. The ground beneath her feet felt soft and uneven as she moved, her breath coming in short, desperate gasps. Every instinct screamed for her to keep moving, to keep running until she could no longer feel the weight of the chase behind her. The investigator was still out there—somewhere. His presence, though not yet seen, hung over her like a storm cloud, dark and foreboding. She could feel it, the cold sweat on her brow, the unshakable sense of dread that had settled deep in her chest.

The moon barely broke through the dense canopy of leaves above, casting only small patches of light onto the forest floor. Elle didn't know how much farther she had gone, but she was certain she wasn't out of danger yet. They were still coming for her.

She had escaped the cabin, the investigator's voice still ringing in her ears as he called for her to surrender. No. She couldn't go back. She couldn't let them catch her again. She had to keep moving.

Her legs burned from the relentless sprint, her body aching with the strain. But she didn't dare stop. Not yet.

She moved through the trees, staying close to the trunks, using the thick foliage to shield herself. The underbrush was dense here, slowing her down with every step. But she had to stay hidden. Every step she took felt like it was one step closer to freedom, yet every sound in the distance made her jump. Were they getting closer?

Her mind raced, trying to formulate a plan. She couldn't just keep running—they would catch up eventually. She needed to think, to find a way out of this. But what was left? Where could she hide? They knew her name. They knew who she was.

Noah's betrayal flashed through her mind, the way his eyes had shifted when he admitted everything. He had been a part of the deception from the very beginning. The man she had trusted, the man who had seemed like an anchor in a storm, had been working for Ethan the whole time. He had been lying to her.

Elle's breath hitched at the thought. Noah had said he was trying to protect her, but now, she wasn't sure who or what to trust anymore. He had failed her. He had let her down.

And now, as the cold wind rustled through the trees, she

realized something even worse: she was alone. The forest had swallowed her whole, and for the first time in a long while, Elle couldn't see the way out.

With a sharp intake of breath, she stumbled to a halt, feeling her heart thunder in her chest. Her eyes darted around the forest, but it was too quiet. The footsteps had stopped. Had they found her? Had the investigator figured out where she had gone? Or was this another trick of the mind, the deepening panic that clouded her every thought?

No. They wouldn't have caught her this quickly.

Elle's eyes flicked to the dark path ahead of her, barely visible through the overgrown thicket of leaves and branches. She had to keep moving, but she couldn't allow herself to make any more mistakes. Her mind raced, trying to find a plan, any plan that could give her an edge. Think, Elle.

And then, in the distance, she saw something—a flicker of light through the trees. A soft glow, barely visible through the thick night. It wasn't a streetlight, not the kind she'd grown accustomed to seeing in town. It was something different—something strange.

Elle's heart skipped a beat. She knew it could be a trap. It could be anything. But it was a chance. And right now, it was the only chance she had. She had no choice but to investigate.

Moving as quietly as she could, Elle crept toward the light, her body low to the ground, every sense alert. The sound of her

The Runaway Bride

breathing seemed too loud in the silence of the woods, and every crack of a twig felt like it would give her away. But she pushed forward, knowing that if she stopped, if she hesitated even for a second, she'd lose whatever advantage she had left.

As she approached, the light grew brighter, revealing a small clearing ahead. There, nestled between the trees, was a cabin—old, dilapidated, but still standing. The windows were boarded up, and the roof sagged slightly, but there was no mistaking it. This was a place to hide.

Elle's pulse quickened. She didn't know if she could trust the safety of this cabin, but she didn't have much time to weigh her options. She had to make a choice now.

The wind picked up, and Elle's skin prickled with the sudden chill. She reached for the door handle, her fingers trembling as they brushed against the cold metal. The door was old, rusted, but when she turned it, it creaked open.

Elle stepped inside, holding her breath as she took in the darkness of the room. The faint scent of mildew and old wood filled the air, but there was something more—something heavier in the atmosphere. She couldn't quite place it, but the hairs on the back of her neck stood on end.

The room was sparse, empty except for a single chair near a small fireplace. The only sound was the wind outside, the branches of the trees rustling in the distance. She couldn't see much in the dark, but she knew there was no turning back now. The woods were too dangerous, too open. If they found her out here, she would have no chance of escape.

Elle made her way deeper into the cabin, moving quietly, her senses heightened. Where was the light coming from? The source was somewhere inside, hidden in the back of the room. She had to find it. She had to make sure she wasn't walking into a trap.

Her eyes scanned the room. The fireplace was cold, but the small flicker of light in the corner caught her attention. A lamp—barely visible in the corner of the room, flickering softly as though someone had just turned it on. Elle's stomach twisted.

Someone was here.

Her heart raced. She should've known better. This wasn't just some random, abandoned cabin. This was a place that someone knew. Someone had been here recently.

And then, she heard it. A sound.

A door creaked, faint footsteps echoing through the cabin. Elle froze, her heart nearly leaping out of her chest. She wasn't alone.

The steps grew louder, and in that moment, Elle's mind screamed one word: Run.

But she didn't. She couldn't. Not yet.

The Runaway Bride

A figure emerged from the shadows, a silhouette in the dim light. The unmistakable figure of Noah.

"Elle," he said, his voice soft but urgent. "Please. You need to listen to me."

Elle's breath caught in her throat, a wave of disbelief washing over her. She had hoped to never see him again, but here he was—standing in front of her, his eyes filled with emotion. She had thought she had escaped. But now, she wasn't so sure. She didn't know what to think, or what to do.

"Noah," Elle said, her voice shaky with the weight of everything. "What are you doing here? What—what do you want from me?"

"I'm not here to hurt you," he said quickly, his hands held out, palms facing her. "I've been trying to protect you, to keep you safe. But I can't stop what's coming, Elle. I can't stop Ethan from getting to you."

Elle's heart thudded painfully in her chest. Ethan.

She took a step back, a part of her refusing to believe it. "No," she whispered. "You're lying to me. You were part of this all along. You—"

"I never wanted this for you," Noah cut in, his voice pained, his expression filled with frustration. "I was trying to protect you. You need to understand, Elle, Ethan—he's dangerous. And now, they're getting closer. You need to trust me."

Elle stood there, frozen, her thoughts spinning in chaos. Everything she had known, everything she had fought for, was now in question. Was Noah truly trying to help her, or was this another game he was playing?

"I don't trust you anymore," Elle said coldly, shaking her head. "I can't. Not after everything."

"No, please." Noah stepped forward, his hand reaching out as though to touch her, but Elle stepped back, her body tense with fear and anger. She couldn't let him near her.

"I'm sorry, but I can't keep running with you anymore," Elle said, her voice hard. "I won't let you drag me back into this mess. I won't be anyone's pawn."

Noah's face fell. He seemed to struggle with the words, his expression shifting as though he were trying to find the right thing to say. But nothing he could say would change what had already been done.

And in that moment, Elle realized the terrifying truth: She was alone.

The walls closed in as she stood in the dimly lit cabin, her past crashing in on her, with no way to escape it. She had been running for so long, and yet, every step she took seemed to bring her closer to the same conclusion.

The nightmare had never truly ended.

It was just beginning.

Twenty

Breaking Point

The air in the cabin was thick with tension. Elle's heart pounded in her chest, her breath shallow and uneven. The flickering light from the lamp cast long, haunting shadows against the walls, distorting the room into something unfamiliar, something menacing. Noah stood before her, his presence so familiar and yet so foreign now.

Everything about him had changed in her eyes. The kindness, the warmth—those moments of vulnerability they shared—they were just illusions. His hands were still outstretched, desperate, but Elle couldn't make herself reach back. Not anymore. She couldn't even look at him without feeling the weight of the betrayal crashing over her once more. He had been a part of the plan all along. She had been a pawn, caught in a game she didn't even understand until it was too late.

"You need to listen to me," Noah said again, his voice cracking slightly, as though the words themselves were a struggle. He stepped closer, but Elle took another step back, her eyes narrowing.

"No, Noah," she said, the words coming out sharper than she meant. "I don't need to listen to you. You've had your chance."

His face tightened, and the frustration in his eyes was clear, but there was something else too—guilt. It almost felt like he was fighting with himself, trying to find the words to explain, to make her understand, but she wasn't sure there were words left that could fix this. "You don't get it," he said, his voice more urgent now. "I'm trying to help you. I'm trying to protect you from what's coming. Ethan will—"

"Ethan," Elle hissed. The name tasted like poison on her tongue, the very thought of him making her skin crawl. "Don't you dare say his name to me. Don't you dare pretend like you're trying to protect me. You've been a part of this mess from the beginning. You lied to me. You—" She couldn't finish the sentence, her words cutting off as the flood of emotions overwhelmed her. Anger, fear, betrayal—it all came rushing to the surface.

"I didn't want this, Elle," Noah said, his voice quieter now, almost pleading. "I didn't want you to get caught up in it. But it's too late. It's all too far gone." His gaze flickered to the window, his eyes darting nervously, and Elle could feel the unease in his posture. It wasn't just guilt. It was something more. Fear. Desperation. He knew what was coming.

Elle took another step back, her mind racing. She couldn't stay here, couldn't stay in this cabin with him. But where would she go? She had no one left to trust. No safe places, no way to escape this nightmare. The forest around her was dark, unforgiving. And the truth was, no matter where she went, they would always be one step behind her.

"We can't keep running, Elle," Noah said, his voice softer now, almost resigned. "You can't keep running. They'll find you. And when they do, it'll be over."

Elle clenched her fists at her sides, the anger building up again, fierce and uncontrollable. She wanted to scream, to shout at him, to let all of the pain and betrayal pour out of her in one violent outburst. But something stopped her. A voice, quiet and insistent, told her to hold on. To think.

"You don't know what they'll do to me, Noah," Elle said, her voice low, cold. "You don't know what they've done to me already. You're just as bad as them."

Noah looked pained, like her words were knives digging into his chest. His jaw tightened, his fists clenching at his sides, but he didn't argue. Instead, he turned toward the window, his eyes scanning the darkness outside.

"They're close," he said quietly, his voice tense. "They've found us. They'll be here soon."

Elle froze, her stomach sinking. She could feel the weight of his words like a cold fist in her gut. It was over.

She didn't know what to do, where to go. She had spent so long running, so long trying to find some kind of safety, only to realize that there was no such thing. The people who had been chasing her—Ethan, the investigator, even Noah—were all part of the same twisted game. A game where she was nothing more than a piece to be moved around.

"Please," Noah said again, his voice barely above a whisper. He turned to face her, his eyes filled with a mixture of desperation and regret. "You don't have to do this. Let me help you. Let me make this right."

Elle shook her head. "No." The word was firm, final. "You can't make this right. You can't fix what you've done."

There was a long pause, the silence between them thick with unspoken words. The tension in the air felt suffocating, and for the first time in a long while, Elle felt her resolve start to waver. Her body was exhausted, her mind frayed from the constant running, the constant fear. But there was still something deep inside her, something stubborn, that refused to give up. She wasn't going to let them win. Not now. Not ever.

She glanced toward the window again, her mind racing for some kind of plan, some kind of escape. The cabin felt like it was closing in on her, the walls pressing tighter with every passing second. She had to leave. She had to move.

"We need to go," Elle said suddenly, her voice steady despite the panic surging through her. "We can't stay here. They'll find us."

Noah looked at her, his eyes filled with confusion, but there was a flicker of something else—something that looked like hope. "Elle, you're not alone in this," he said softly. "I can help you. We can—"

"No." Elle's voice was sharp. "I'm not trusting anyone anymore. Not you. Not anyone."

Noah's face fell. He opened his mouth as if to speak, but Elle didn't give him a chance. She turned on her heel and headed toward the door. "Stay out of my way," she said over her shoulder, her voice cold and resolute.

Noah didn't try to stop her. He didn't move. And for a moment, Elle felt the weight of his silence, like a thousand unspoken words between them. But she couldn't dwell on that now. She couldn't afford to.

The door creaked as Elle pushed it open, the night air rushing in, cold and heavy. She stepped out onto the porch, her eyes scanning the darkness, looking for any sign of movement. Nothing.

But she couldn't shake the feeling. The feeling that they were still out there. That they were always going to be out there.

Elle walked down the stairs, her eyes darting back to Noah, who was still standing in the doorway, watching her with an unreadable expression. She couldn't stay here. She couldn't keep running from him, from the truth. But she couldn't stay with him, either. She couldn't trust him.

The Runaway Bride

"I'll find a way out," Elle said, her voice barely above a whisper. "I'll do it alone."

Noah said nothing. His eyes lingered on her for a moment longer, but then, without a word, he disappeared back into the cabin.

Elle didn't look back. She couldn't.

She stepped into the darkness of the woods, her feet heavy with the weight of her choices. The forest stretched out in front of her, endless and unknowable. But somewhere in the distance, she could see the faint outline of a road. A place she could go. A place where she could finally disappear.

But no matter where she went, she knew they would follow.

And this time, she wasn't sure how long she could keep running.

www.ingramcontent.com/pod-product-compliance
Lightning Source LLC
LaVergne TN
LVHW011946070526
838202LV00054B/4816